stop saying I'm fine

"There's a sentence right in the middle of this book where Taylor writes, 'At its core, the spiritual journey is one of God continually welcoming us home, not only to a truer version of him but also to a truer version of ourselves.' To me, that's the heart of this book. But here's what makes it beautiful: Taylor doesn't just *tell* us that truth; she *shows* us that truth in her own story. It is a story both painful and beautiful. But in telling it, what Taylor does is invite others into that same journey—back home, to both God and to ourselves."

—**Josh Rutledge,** Vice President of Spiritual Development, Liberty University

"For anyone who struggles with anxiety and has experienced the pain of feeling misunderstood or judged by fellow believers, Taylor's heartfelt words will be a soothing balm to their soul as she becomes the friend to lead them out of their darkness. Through her vulnerability, honesty, and personal stories, readers will uncover the healing and peace they've desperately been seeking and leave the fear, isolation, and shame of anxiety in the past."

—**Tracie Miles,** author and writing coach

"This book is a gift of jagged edges. It's a gift because many of us don't know how to process our deepest pain, but Taylor walks it with dignity, honesty, and courage. This is a beautifully raw distillation of what it means to daily choose to walk back to Jesus and the arms he keeps open. Taylor uses her experiences to write with a perceptive understanding of the human–divine tension. This book opened my eyes to what it means to encounter a grace that is gripping and unrelenting."

—**Dr. Mary Lowe,** Online Associate Dean, Liberty University, School of Divinity

"In this book, Taylor Murray recounts the struggle with anxiety and anorexia that led her to reject self-sufficiency and embrace the grace of the cross. She invites readers to think deeply about the roots of our need to be 'fine,' even when we're not. Her honest and hopeful story highlights the goodness of God in our pain and lights the way for others in today's challenging environment."

—**Steve Richardson,** President, Pioneers-USA

"Taylor's tender heart for those who are suffering has led her to write a breathtakingly beautiful invitation to know God more intimately. Dripping with both Scripture and vulnerability, *Stop Saying I'm Fine* will reach the hidden places of your heart and soul and provide a sturdy handhold on your journey to deeper healing and freedom."

—**Elizabeth Trotter,** author of *Serving Well*, editor-in-chief of the missions website A Life Overseas

"Taylor's vulnerable sharing of her own story gives courage for all ages to press into God's invitation to be his beloved. She has done a magnificent job of intertwining her battle with anxiety and wrestling with God's goodness. Taylor writes to her generation but I believe has a message for all to hear. I would highly recommend this book to anyone who has struggled with any form of anxiety."

—**Carolyn Foster,** Certified Spiritual Director

"*Stop Saying I'm Fine* is a must-read for anyone who wants to find meaning and healing in his or her struggles with pain and anxiety. Taylor's honest and compelling personal story coupled with her incredible writing will keep you captivated from beginning to end."

—**David Nasser,** author and President of For Others Collective

"High praise for this resource that is welcomed by struggling individuals battling anxiety and caring professionals alike. In culture and church, Taylor challenges us to offer compassionate courage as we look behind the masks of those living with this *all too pervasive disorder*. As she authentically shares her journey, we are given both her insight *and* permission to shed pretense and performance—replacing them with grace leading to triumph, and truth leading to freedom."

—**Dorcas Harbin,** Executive Vice President of One Another Ministries, Intl

"In *Stop Saying I'm Fine*, Taylor Murray generously invites us into her authentic and life-changing journey from the isolating bondage to anxiety to the practical freedom of grace in community. Woven throughout the book, she boldly shares the skill of learning self-awareness as well as becoming aware of God's loving presence. These two skills will unlock the path to Christ-centered transformation and clear a path to experiencing beauty, hope, and freedom regardless of circumstance."

—**Wendy Adamson,** career global worker, spiritual director, and soul care provider for global workers

stop
saying
i'm fine

FINDING STILLNESS WHEN
ANXIETY SCREAMS

taylor joy murray

LEAFWOOD
PUBLISHERS
an imprint of Abilene Christian University Press

STOP SAYING I'M FINE

Finding Stillness When Anxiety Screams

LEAFWOOD
P U B L I S H E R S
an imprint of Abilene Christian University Press

Copyright © 2022 by Taylor Joy Murray

ISBN 978-1-68426-139-0

Printed in the United States of America

Scripture quotations noted NIV are from The Holy Bible, New International Version® NIV®. Copyright © 1973, 1978, 1984, 2011 by Biblica, Inc.™ Used by permission. All rights reserved worldwide.

Scripture quotations noted TPT are from The Passion Translation®. Copyright © 2017, 2018, 2020 by Passion & Fire Ministries, Inc. Used by permission. All rights reserved. ThePassionTranslation.com.

Scripture quotations noted NLT are taken from the New Living Translation, Copyright ©1996, 2004, 2007 by Tyndale House Foundation. Used by permission of Tyndale House Publishers, Inc., Carol Stream, IL 60188. All rights reserved.

Scripture quotations noted *The Message* taken from *The Message*. Copyright © 1993, 1994, 1995, 1996, 2000, 2001, 2002. Used by permission of NavPress Publishing Group.

Cataloging-in-Publication Data is on file at the Library of Congress, Washington, DC.

Cover design by ThinkPen Design, LLC
Interior text design by Strong Design, Sandy Armstrong

Leafwood Publishers is an imprint of Abilene Christian University Press
ACU Box 29138
Abilene, Texas 79699

1-877-816-4455
www.leafwoodpublishers.com

22 23 24 25 26 27 28 / 7 6 5 4 3 2 1

"Nothing in all creation is so like God as stillness."

—Meister Eckhart

Contents

Note to Readers 9

Introduction   God, Will You Please Fix Me?. 11

part one

Chapter One   Picture-Perfect Prisons. 19

Chapter Two   People Paralysis 31

Chapter Three   The Voice in My Head. 41

Chapter Four   But How Do I Even Get through Today?. 51

Chapter Five   An Invitation to the Sacred Space 61

part two

Chapter Six   Bleeding in a Thousand Places. 75

Chapter Seven   The Language of the Wounded Heart 87

Chapter Eight   Running from Myself. 97

Chapter Nine   Scrubbed Clean and Crawling. 107

Chapter Ten   Waking Up to the Color 117

part three

Chapter Eleven   God's Whisper to the Waiting Heart 131

Chapter Twelve   Walking on Wasted Grace 143

Chapter Thirteen Coexisting with Uncertainty. 157

Chapter Fourteen Becoming the Beloved. 167

Chapter Fifteen   Becoming Us. 179

Notes 189

Note to Readers

Every chapter of this book comes from a deep place, birthed from my own pain, desperation, and spiritual wrestling. It's the slow outworking of my own journey with anxiety. Although I've grounded my work in the research of psychologists, psychiatrists, and therapists, I am specifically writing from a spiritual-emotional perspective. There are some forms of entrenched anxiety that are anchored so deeply in our bodies' chemistry that professional and medical intervention are necessary. This has been a part of my story, too. I certainly do not believe anxiety is solely a spiritual problem, but spirituality has been an integral part of my healing. It's felt daunting and risky to try to put words to this journey, requiring me to travel inside myself in an attempt to make sense of my story. But as we walk this road together, I pray I've opened up a pathway for you to do the same. I pray that as you settle into this process and begin to peer inward, you'll discover that the healing you long for isn't as distant as it may seem.

God, Will You Please Fix Me?

Have you ever wondered if everyone else understands how to live the Christian life but you? For most of my life, I didn't dare say this out loud. It was a sense that lingered in me for years, which eventually led to a slow and gradual unraveling.

I made a confession of faith at a young age, and I soon realized that my prayer hadn't fixed my pain, shame, and sin patterns. But I was a little girl who could win a prize for pretending I was fine when I was not . . . when all the unspoken pain and stuffed emotions felt like shards of glass in my stomach. Over years of crushed hopes and cutting reality, a fog rolled in. An inner dullness brought with it a silent but steady trickling of doubts and unsettling questions. What did Jesus mean when he promised us full life?

Spiritually, it might feel like you've slammed into a solid, impenetrable wall.

I know that place. I've banged my fists against this wall, only to feel more stuck. More alone. Life pauses here, at this mark in time where you can't seem to move forward. I felt fragmented, caught off guard by a sense of plunging inadequacy. Those frightening thoughts can swirl in at the most unexpected moments—is it even possible to be a Christian and feel like this?

If you're like me, you've tried reading your Bible. Praying more. Vowing to God that you'll do better. But as you loop that endless cycle of resolved effort and repeated defeat, exhaustion seeps in. Eventually, you give up. You disengage to save yourself the pain of more disappointment. You feel foolish for trying, for even hoping things could be different. Slowly, your soul stiffens, crusting over and forming in you a silent shell of skeptical cynicism.

Now all those things just seem like glossy practices that good Christians do, but they ricochet ineffectively off a sense of ever-widening emptiness in you.

We live in a spiritual environment that celebrates exuberant beginnings and emphasizes victorious endings, but what if we feel hopelessly stuck in the in-between? And where do Jesus's promises of wholeness and freedom fit into life's often excruciating unraveling in these middle places? His promises can feel confusing, if not cruel.

> I am a Christian who wholeheartedly believes in Jesus, but I've often doubted if the healing unleashed by his scarred and broken body runs deep enough to heal the scarred and broken parts of me.

The first time I took communion, I stood barely taller than the pew in front of me. I held the bread carefully in an open palm. The cup was tiny and plastic, filled with grape juice. As I partook, head bowed, I also held a deep-seated belief internally. An untainted narrative, knit into my thinking, that shaped my perception of reality: *The world is safe, and I am whole and loved and free. I will live a good life for God, and God will be good to me.*

This is the little-girl line I once believed.

The truth is, I seemed to sin and struggle more after that day. And the events that cascaded into my life didn't always feel good. The pain was often breathtaking. Gradually, the reality of our world caused me to question, *Is God really good?* The bread and cup slowly felt less personal. Less weighty. Less final. Less full of wonder and forgiveness and promise. Less reminiscent of Jesus's sacrifice, and more like bleak reminders of healing and freedom detached from my reality. Was something wrong with me?

Slowly, my little-girl perception of God, myself, and how the world was supposed to be fissured and cracked, and then shattered completely. The more pain and rejection and loss wound like a black cord through the fabric of my life, the more the lies slipped in. Those tugging whispers of sin and shame yanked the grace right out of my soul.

Christ's sacrifice didn't really work.

You're not truly free.

God's grace doesn't apply here.

You aren't good enough for God's love.

As our society has taught us, I hid all the pain behind a happy exterior. I'd discovered that our church services are frequently filled with smiling faces, with pews of people who appeared like they had their acts together. Was pretending the only way to belong? I knew this was not fully true, but it often felt true. I grew accustomed to promoting a filtered version of myself. The more entangled I became in the pain of past wounds and everyday struggles, the louder that voice grew. *Maybe freedom is real for others but certainly not for me.*

Later, there was a time when I sat in a church service, hollow and vacant-eyed. The ache inside me was so lacerating, it hurt to breathe. *Oh, Jesus.* Was I the only one? The shame weighed heavy. No hope anymore. Only woundedness. *Will you please just fix me?* That was my silent cry to a God who seemed far away. The bread and the cup were stale symbols of sacrificial healing and wholeness unavailable to me. As everyone else partook together, I got up and left the room.

If you've ever struggled with these questions, if you've ever felt stuck or confused or deeply alone in your faith, this book is for you. The day I left church midway through communion, I was in a dark place. A lonely place. I truly believed I was the only one. The Enemy likes to tell us that. Although our experiences are different, this road of life we're walking is surprisingly similar. Just different landscapes, threaded together by our own personal experiences of pain. Can we journey for a bit together?

There is a lot of noise in our churches today. Voices ring about checklists and church services and altar calls, and promise shortcuts and easy routes to linear change and shiny spirituality. But I'm learning that the spiritual journey Jesus invites us to is so much more than this. Deeper than this. Messier than this. Longer than this. The hand Jesus extends welcomes us to a walk that can't be mastered by ten steps or to-do lists. I am the first to admit that control feels safer and releasing completely sounds risky. Terrifying, actually. But when I try to control my faith, I find myself existing merely on the fringes of life, fastened to a shallow, static, and artificial exterior.

In these pages, I want to sit unhurriedly together in a part of spirituality less talked about. A quieter, more hidden, less discovered space, where we'll both have permission to breathe freely. Inhale grace, exhale honesty. To take off our happy smiles and ask the raw questions of the heart. Wrestling is welcome here. It's a place where spiritual transformation isn't solely about moving forward, but about looking back. It's about an unrushed process, a slow and fluid unfolding. Spiritual transformation is also about going back to the child inside of you and tracing the threads of pain. The loss, devastation, and heartache that have leaked into your life and snaked their way through the making of you.

> I've often been told that spiritual intimacy is all about knowing God. While this is absolutely true, it's also about knowing ourselves.

At first, this might sound odd, even self-absorbed. I thought so too. But when I look at other relationships in my life, I find this dynamic resoundingly true: relational depth occurs, not only as I get to know the other person but as I get to know myself too. God longs for us to know him, experientially, through the channel of our own hearts. Digging deep into ourselves, then, becomes the avenue to a deeper walk with him.

I often recoil from revisiting my story or sitting with the unfixed parts of myself. Our world moves at such an accelerated rate, and I don't naturally feel comfortable with slow, quiet, or messy. Those words aren't popular and rarely valued in our society, and I constantly feel a counteractive pull. These interior places scare me, so I usually try to move on quickly. Forget the past and focus on the future. But I'm gradually learning what it looks like to be present with my aches, my wounds, and my questions. Here, God is most present with me.

It's typically during red lights or sleepless nights or when I'm brushing my teeth that the thoughts and feelings come. Those pangs and insecurities from recent events that are so often tied to formative parts of my past. I'm learning to breathe deeply in these moments and to linger here with Jesus. Over the last few years, as I've allowed those feelings to come—and when I've processed them out with him and trusted others, they've become the pathway through my spiritual stuckness. The road that has led to real and lasting change. To the fuller freedom that Jesus promised.

A wise woman once told me, "When we stuff our pain to the basement of our souls, it will deal with us until we allow God to deal with it." In order to understand the deeper things of God, we must be willing to peer unflinchingly into the deepest parts of ourselves. God has promised to make his home in us, and part of the spiritual journey is coming home to ourselves.

So, will you join me as we turn inward? Descend the winding, sometimes wobbling, staircase of our stories all the way down to the basement of our souls. That is where the real us will begin to meet the real God. We'll find that when we face our stuffed pain, inviting all these wounded places within us together, we'll experience him in the depths of our being and discover who we most truly are.

part one

CHAPTER ONE

Picture-Perfect Prisons

I sat on a gray-tiled floor and stared numbly at the tiny sliver of light through the crack of the bathroom door. The darkness around me and *in* me felt so heavy . . . like the feel of gravity when you're falling. Dragging you lower and lower at a frightening rate, and the only direction you can see is *down*. Inwardly frozen, I focused every ounce of mental capacity I had left to draw the next lungful of air.

Breathe. Just breathe.

Legs tucked up to my chest, I wrapped my arms around my knees. Fists clenched and knuckles white, I willed myself to inhale. *One, two, three.* And then a long, shaky exhale.

Have you ever promised yourself that you are done with that certain struggle, that old habit, that relentless insecurity (like, really done), only for it to suddenly resurface with overwhelming force later on? Me too. I had graduated high school five months prior to this bout on the bathroom floor. Cap and gown in hand, I'd also determined—at a more subconscious level—that another kind of graduation was long overdue: I was *over* fighting with fear, and with food. I was about to catch a flight to Zurich and then a ferry to an international Bible college nestled in the lakeside city of Friedrichshafen, Germany.

Anxiety and disordered eating? Neither of them were invited. Definitely not. These internal struggles had silently snuck into my life a few years earlier, dancing into my mind during a difficult season, and then digging their heels into my thinking patterns, thought processes, and most instinctive nervous system responses. But today, I was declaring *no more*. They were not welcome here any longer. I packed my suitcase and hoped somehow a change of scenery would loosen the grip of these sicknesses that had been sucking the life out of me for too long.

> Why do sentences like that sound so logical when we think them and then seem so ridiculously silly in reality?

When I arrived in Germany, I was immediately plunged into a plethora of new and once-in-a-lifetime opportunities. Hikes in the Alps. Bike rides through vineyards at sunset. Weekday classes and Saturday meanderings through quaint German towns. I backpacked with friends through Paris, Prague, and Rome over Christmas break. Every morning, we'd layer on every piece of clothing we owned to keep warm against the icy European winter. We soon discovered that the cost of travel far exceeded our budgets, which resulted in an often comical and always creative spin to everything. We slept in the cheapest Airbnbs we could find and used our student cards to explore all the attractions cost-free. I posted pictures in front of the Eiffel Tower and the Roman Colosseum.

"How was break?" People asked once we all returned for spring session.

"Great!" I responded with a grin. But I wasn't able to ignore the internal voice growing louder every day and telling me what a fraud I was.

I was definitely not great. I wasn't even remotely okay. Long before that moment on the bathroom floor, I had sensed that I was sliding back into old, supposed-to-have-graduated-from patterns. *But I'm fine, really,* I assured myself. *Everyone has moments, right?* And then I began slipping, here and there. *But I'm just being overly cautious. That slipup doesn't matter.* And progressively, after a litany of small and seemingly insignificant decisions, I was full-on spiraling. As weeks turned into months, panic began to claw at my confidence. I knew, deep in the pit of my stomach, that what was supposed to have been a whimsical vacation had wreaked havoc inside my mind.

One morning in March, when the sun had finally begun to thaw our frozen surroundings, the director's wife (we'll call her G) pulled me aside. With worried eyes, she told me she was concerned about my health. Tears rimmed my eyes as I admitted my recent struggles. I was too scared of how sick I felt to keep pretending otherwise. That afternoon, I didn't protest when she promptly marched me down cobblestoned *Ziegelstrasse* to our neighborhood clinic.

We walked through glass doors into a cold, white-walled office and sat in plastic, hard-backed chairs across from a German female doctor. In the span of a brisk, professional, and fact-only conversation, I was labeled severely anorexic. Although I sat, numb and silent, a lost and wounded part of me screamed inside.

G and I walked back together, and neither of us said much. The weight of my diagnosis was clearly heavy on our minds. As the world ushered in the colors of spring, my deadened spirit seemed strikingly out of place. We strolled past the Bodensee, a lake that wraps around the college campus. My eyes wandered to bare, bony trees clustered around the shoreline. I couldn't help but notice their wintry rebellion against a world that screamed *life*.

I thought of all my pretending lately. How convincingly my plastic smiles and polished prayers had broadcast my own version of spring. But I felt the emptiness of those trees inside.

Back at the dorms, I barely made it up to the second-floor restrooms. I raced to the only stall with a full door and lock. *Thank goodness, it's open.* All that exposure had left me raw. Nowhere else to go to be alone. I closed the door and, after a moment's hesitation, flipped the light off. With a rush of relief, I finally felt my outside and inside shake hands. I curled up on the floor in a fetal position, lungs convulsing as I heaved precious slivers of air. My eating disorder and anxiety had definitely disregarded my uninviting them.

For over an hour I sat in that dark bathroom stall, locking others out and feeling trapped in my own thoughts.

How could I let this happen?

I feel so alone.

I'm a failure.

Will this ever end?

No one can know about this.

How did I get here?

Who was I anymore?

I ached to crawl out of my own skin. Instead, I was left with my frailty, this anxiety, my inability to escape. I was terrified of this growing darkness that seemed to be swallowing me from the inside. I just wanted to run away. I just wanted to close my eyes and go away, if that was what would bring relief.

And the ironic part was, for so long, I'd been doing just that. For years, I'd been doing everything humanly possible to ignore all the unspoken pain gnawing and festering and swelling. The carefree little girl in me slowly slipped away as I ran from all those frightening and unknown places that exist in each of us. As I ran, I stopped feeling alive. It had become too painful to be with others, too painful to be with myself. No safe place to exist anymore. But, today? I had crashed, unforgivingly, into the reality of myself. As what-ifs and should-haves breathed down my neck, I realized, at that moment, I was most fearful of myself.

Years later, I still struggle to talk about that day. Ten weeks of residential treatment after my semester in Germany and then hundreds of counseling sessions in the last few years, however, have allowed me to sit deeply in my own story and untangle all those emotions warring against each other.

But what was I primarily feeling? Tension.

There was this tension between what I was portraying and what was actually going on inside me. This unsettling dichotomy between my outer and inner worlds. I felt stuck in the middle. And the tension was exhausting.

But I don't think I need to tell you that. I think a deep part of you might feel exhausted, too. You know what it's like when picture-perfect becomes a prison. When you feel trapped inside yourself, with your own personalized poison. And when all your unspoken not-okayness has carved in you an aching and cavernous sense of aloneness.

The crippling anxiety. The secret addiction. The sexual abuse you promised you'd never tell anyone about. That debilitating insecurity. The unhealed hurt. The deep relational wound. The devastating loss. The destructive habit. That lie you've always believed. The family dysfunction. That soul-crushing regret over a life decision you so desperately wish you could undo. Can I tell you something you already know, but maybe don't fully believe yet? Although your story is your own, you aren't the only one. Far from it, friend. My own pain often fogs my ability to see the wounds and scars of others. But sometimes, I'll catch a stranger's eye on a street corner or see the fleeting unguarded expression in the face of a friend. And when I do? I'm stunned by the pain of just one human, shoulders sagging under what feels like a million invisible hurts.

> How often do we present external, everyday versions of ourselves to the world while the weight of unacknowledged wounds and unhealed hurts wears and frays at our souls?

You and I have become adept at concealing pain behind perfected poses. We know what to say and how to say it. How to look and who to portray in order to maintain some semblance of spring, just enough to keep people at a safe distance. Over the years, our world has turned the elusive art of pretending into a socially expected approach to belonging. But the truth is, our filtered selves are ill fitting. They disconnect us from our own hearts. They cause us to feel lost in our buried pain, in the foggy terrains of our own inner worlds. They feel uncomfortable. *Not right.* Slowly, our souls are slipping away. Retreating deep inside us for the overpowering presence of loneliness and shame.

Shame says, "I hate myself."

Shame says, "I am worthless."

Shame says, "I am bad."

Shame says, "I must hide."

As well-known researcher Brené Brown writes, "Shame works like a zoom lens on a camera. When we are feeling shame, the camera is zoomed in tight and all we see is our flawed selves, alone and struggling."[1]

A few days ago, while getting my hair cut, I chatted with my hairdresser. As she finished blow-drying my new cut, she asked if I wanted her to style it.

I responded with a smiling affirmative.

After some expert flat-ironing and back-combing, she spun me around and held up a hand mirror for my viewing. "Time for selfies, right?" she asked with a satisfied grin.

Her natural (and well-grounded!) assumption: on the day that I look nothing like I usually do, I'll take pictures of myself. Choose the best one. Select the shiniest filter. Mull over a caption. And then post it on social media, hoping that others will see this better-than-life version of me and believe that's how I always look. In other words, I'll carefully construct and promote a picture-perfect version of myself, all while my own insecure gaze has never left the zoomed-in, struggling version.

As I sat on that bathroom floor in Germany, I realized I didn't need an iPhone or Instagram account anymore. The filtered version of myself had become who I was in the world. It's who I portrayed. It's who I presented myself to be. Like me, many of us are so accustomed to our shiny layers, our fake smiles, our stuffed pain . . . the skin-deep version of ourselves . . . that we've lost sight of who we are becoming.

We've never discovered who we most deeply are.

I wish we could sit across from one another at a coffee shop, warm drinks in hand, as we begin to process some questions together. Questions that might already be sitting, buried and unanswered, in your soul. I'm not asking that you do anything when you read these questions. Just ponder them. Give yourself permission to feel the pangs of loss they might usher in. When did you and I stop feeling alive? When did the carefree child in us begin to seep away? When did our souls stop feeling safe to come out, to breathe? When did we learn that we must hide all this hurt we feel inside? When did we discover that the world only likes people who keep their internal messiness behind a tidy and perfectly packaged exterior?

Can I tell you something I've learned over the last few years? There is so much more to me than what the world wants me to see, what my past has taught me to believe, and what the Enemy tells me to live by. But his voice can be so undeniably convincing. He'll drop tiny seeds of self-doubt and comparison into my mind. He'll tell me that I'll never measure up, that no one else feels what I do, that vulnerability is too scary, and that the world isn't a safe place for my heart. He usually doesn't have to say much for the insecure, fearful side of me to claim his lies as truth, make up all kinds of false stories, and soon find myself emotionally knotted and tangled inside. In dozens of notoriously subtle ways, the Enemy seeks to widen the gap between our external persona and our inner world. Why? Because in the tension in between, we fall spiritually asleep. We settle for merely scraping the surface of the life God intended.

Instead, we feel stuck in the following anxiety-inducing narrative: I'm not living the life I want to live. I'm not becoming the person I want to be. And perhaps even more painful, I'm not living the life God wants me to live. I'm not becoming the person God wants me to be. This can't be all there is to life.

In that moment on the bathroom floor, I sat and imagined Jesus at a distance, joining me in my vicious stare-down over the zoomed-in version of my struggling self. I imagined him peering over the balcony of heaven with eyes of judgment, an occasional sigh of disapproval, and a laundry list of all the things I should have done differently. Utterly defeated, I couldn't bring myself to meet his gaze. But a small, fragile part of me wondered, *What does Jesus think about me when I break? Where is he when I feel shattered into an unfixable pile of pieces?*

Although it certainly didn't feel like it to me, Jesus *was* close by.

I would understand later that there was no trace of disappointment in his gaze. He was the one giving me each lungful of air. Crouching low on the bathroom floor, he was holding me. Whispering love. Weeping with me. Speaking to me.

We all have some version of a bathroom-floor moment, don't we? I know from experience: it can be easy to sink into the shame, to paint judgment or disapproval on his face. I often feel he is so unreachable. But as I've processed these moments of life, I've realized that the ring of his voice is less clouded by disappointment and more cloaked with a warm and grace-filled invitation. An invitation to a growth journey with him.

This invitation is always and resoundingly open to us every moment of our lives. But oftentimes it's when we're brought low, crushed beneath the world's chaos, and attuned to the silent undercurrents of our inner aches, pains, and questions that we can hear his offer extended.

> What if broken, on the bathroom floor, is
> actually the best place to be?

Only by sitting still, in the echoing darkness of your own wounded heart, can you hear God's whispered invitation to wholeness. It's an invitation to peer inward and let the pain come out. It's an invitation to untangle the past and create space for change and healing. It's an invitation to a deeper kind of becoming. If you feel like you're at the end of yourself, can I lean in and gently tell you something? The place where you are isn't hopeless. It's not unredeemable. You're not beyond repair. The opposite, actually. It's where the journey begins.

The apostle Paul began his own growth journey after encountering Jesus on the road to Damascus. What better example is there of someone crashing into the reality of themselves? As he lay blinded on the roadside, his eyes were opened to the truth. The story he had been telling himself about life, God, and the world did not align with reality. Externally, he was a rising star, a religious expert. In actuality? He was a persecutor, a murderer. What tension he must have felt internally. He wrote the following reminder in his letter to the Galatians, as if he recognized in advance its necessity for generations to come: "It is for freedom that Christ has set us free" (Gal. 5:1 NIV).

Jesus didn't sacrifice his life for us to merely skim the surface of abundance. He longs for us to plunge into the depths of rich, vibrant, and genuine lives. Right now, he's inviting you into:

> a full, adventurous, overflowing walk with him;
> deep, abiding peace;
> healing;
> rooted authenticity in whom he has created you to be;
> vibrant passion and creativity;
> delight in the daily rhythms of life;
> strong and steadfast relationships;
> confident hope;
> laughter;
> the joy of being known; and
> a purpose and mission in life.

Actually living this unidealized life can sometimes seem far away. Removed from reality. Discouragingly distant. For many of us, this kind of freedom can feel unattainable. So we alternate between shiny church pews and darkened bathroom stalls, feeling stuck and stagnant and fake. We're not sure how to move forward or change. So we keep on smiling and pretending we're fine, because a deep part of us believes God only likes the tidy and perfectly packaged version of ourselves too.

But right there in the middle of our unspoken brokenness, Jesus is calling. He's asking us to come out of hiding. To be honest with ourselves, and with him. The most important journey of our lives is the one we can choose to take inside ourselves with him. That's what this growth journey is all about: discovering the true God as we discover our true selves. Change comes as we settle into the process, rather than just wishing for the destination.

So, will you join me on this path?

I can't promise it will be easy, but I can promise it will radically transform you.

It won't change your life, but it will change the way you live and think . . . and even breathe.

If your answer is yes, let's lean into the closing of another kind of gap: the one between who you think you are and who God created you to be.

That's the point of this book. Learning how to walk this healing journey, together.

CHAPTER TWO

People Paralysis

Eventually, I picked myself up off the bathroom floor, flipped on the light, and quietly unlocked the door. Laughter spilled from the hallway as other students meandered toward the cafeteria for dinner. The thought of sitting around a table of happy, smiling faces flooded me with another sickening wave of anxiety. Running to the bathroom sink, I gripped its porcelain rim with clammy fingers and dry-heaved. I felt battle worn from the inside out. Pummeled with an onslaught of overstuffed and unexpressed emotions.

Sometimes reality hits with a pain so intense that you find yourself pressing into numbness to survive it. Shoulders hunched over the bathroom sink, faucet running, my body pulsated with a wild sense of fear that felt nearly debilitating. I splashed icy water over swollen eyes, inhaled deeply, and surrendered with a slow and steady slide into a pit of emotional nothingness. Something inside me knew the only way to live through any of this was to go to sleep to all of it.

Consciously steeling myself with a synthetic smile, I would stay that way—hollow inside and happy outside—for a long time.

Empty pleasantries and a perfunctory litany of *I'm fine*s became my primary means of defense from any unwelcome exposure. From that evening on, I was careful to nod at all the appropriate times. Laugh when I was supposed to. Talk just enough so I wouldn't appear too quiet. Operating with the mechanical movements of a robot, I felt detached from my own body.

Never had I been in such close proximity with others, and never had I felt more guarded and alone. Is it possible to ache with loneliness in one moment and then purposefully avoid eye contact, especially with a familiar face, in the next? Everyone else appeared completely fine. *What was wrong with me?* Over the next few months, I mastered the art of hiding inside myself. Anxiously biting my nails until my fingertips were raw, I was terrified of being discovered. I dragged myself numbly through each day and lingered awake at night, staring at the ceiling and feeling sucked into a darkness I couldn't control.

I didn't realize how prevalent anxiety is among our generation until a few years later. Now I see it everywhere I look. Our generation is sick with it. Consumed by it. In bondage to it. I know what all three of those feel like. Anxiety curls suffocating fingers around every single part of our lives, disrupting our individual stories, our thought patterns, and our self-concepts. It reshapes the way that we engage in relationships and even the way we inhabit our bodies. Anxiety can have a crippling effect, hijacking our emotions and silently communicating to our bodies that we are unsafe, threatened, helpless, and abandoned.

> Anxiety tells a terrifying narrative about our
> lives and causes us to feel disconnected
> from ourselves, others, and God.

My struggles with anxiety and anorexia have filled me with inexplicable shame. Not only did I feel like something was wrong with me, but I felt I was doing something wrong. Those two beliefs are the primary narratives of shame. Much of the latter belief can be traced back to messages I heard about anxiety in the church, which often promoted prayer and trust as the Christian solution to my problem with anxiety. I've heard it preached from pulpits that casting my anxiety on God (1 Pet. 5:7), as the apostle Peter wrote, is the spiritual course of action. So I've prayed until there were no words left. I've repented and wept and asked for healing over and over again.

But when I'm locked inside a church's bathroom stall, white-knuckled and gasping for air, when my stomach is knotted and I feel the nausea rising, casting my anxiety on God is the last thing I'm thinking about. I don't know where I am or what direction I'm going or where any of this is coming from. I'm just trying to breathe. As years passed, I began to realize that the church, where I first encountered joy, didn't seem to have a place for pain. Did God not have a place for my pain either? Why did he feel so distant? My desperate pleas slowly subsided into a simple, aching question.

God, I don't understand. Why aren't you healing me?

It was easy to come to conclusions fringed with defeat and despair. *I guess I'm just not a good Christian. I guess I just can't do the Christian life like everyone else seemingly can. The prayers I'm praying seem to be bouncing off deaf ears.* I know what it's like to sit in a church pew, faint with pain, and feel so very alone. If you've been told similar things about anxiety, if you've been told anxiety is solely a spiritual problem stemming from a lack of belief, I'm so sorry. Those words can scrape you raw, making you feel defective. Crazy. Less than human. I want to lean in and tell you: anxiety is not a sin.

You are not automatically sinning if you struggle with anxiety. Anxiety is not synonymous with a lack of trust. While prayer and trust can be components of healing, they are not the only answer. When the apostle Peter writes about casting our anxieties on Jesus, he is referring to the sin of worry, not the biological response of anxiety.[1] The biological response of anxiety is deeply entrenched in our thought patterns and experienced in our bodies, and often requires therapeutic, medical, and spiritual components for healing. You are not crazy.

Anxiety is not a sin. However, the coping mechanisms and patterns that can proceed from it, the people we become, and the lives we lead as a result of it can be far from the life God intended for us. The results can be destructive and lead us down dark paths. Anxiety is how our bodies respond to things that we haven't dealt with properly. It's the cold sweat drenching your sheets when you jolt awake, heart thumping and eyes wide. It's that feeling of never being able to quite catch your breath. It's those moments when you're watching the mouth of the person sitting across from you move, but you have absolutely no idea what they're saying. It's that state of being physically present but feeling as if you're living outside of yourself. Our brains are incredibly trustworthy organs. When we experience anxiety in our bodies, we must learn how to gently attune to it rather than stuffing or pushing it away. Our anxiety is trying to tell us something.

> An essential component of healing is going deeper, under the happy smiles and shiny surfaces of our lives and into the hidden and stuffed emotions.

That's what this inward journey is all about. Diving beneath the surface of our anxiety into the pain of our experiences. We know something feels off inside. And it's those feelings we constantly try to manage, while maintaining a polished exterior.

Psychiatrist Scott Peck defines mental health as "dedication to reality at all costs."[2] Without understanding ourselves and how our experiences have shaped us, we will never be able to see reality truthfully. We currently view everything and everyone, including God and ourselves, through the lens of the past. Understanding the deeper story of our experiences brings clarity to the ways we are operating and the thoughts we are thinking today. We need an infusion of truth into the places of our anxiety. And this only comes with a commitment to honesty and an opening up to the raw blade of self-awareness. But honesty is scary. Sometimes I'd just rather not know the truth.

Therapist and author Sissy Goff describes anxiety as overestimating the threat and underestimating ourselves and our ability to cope.[3] It's our body's biological response to emotional stimuli, tightening your muscles, flooding your mind with unintelligible static, and disrupting your breathing. This kind of anxiety is paralyzing. An automatic biological response to danger, anxiety numbs our bodies when our nervous systems indicate a sudden overload of emotions: "We can't take anymore!" When these neurological alarms sound, our bodies instinctively respond by shutting down, disconnecting, and withdrawing emotionally.

My physical responses of anxiety are easy to identify. I can recognize in myself the tightened muscles, the paralyzing panic, and the spiraling thoughts. However, in moments of heightened anxiety, my deeper fear (the root of these physical symptoms) is not as easily identifiable. I can often find myself flooded with anxiety or panic without understanding why. My confusion adds to my angst and frustration. Why am I feeling this way? Those deeper fears are difficult to distinguish, especially when connected to more subtle and ambiguous threats. That's why we have to turn inward, listening to our thoughts, revisiting our stories, and seeking to identify those fears, patterns, and beliefs that can trigger our bodies' biological responses.

So many of us live in bondage to fear. The pain slithering through our childhoods, and the wounding and tension in our relationships help shape these fears. Experiences of trauma often reset our bodies to interpret the world as a terrifying and unsafe place.[4] We can wrestle against ourselves, fearing our own compulsive and sometimes destructive tendencies. We fear the future, unsure of the right decisions and uncertain outcomes. We are plagued with worry over financial stability and job security. Many of us live with constant anxiety about terrorism, natural disasters, and pandemics, feeling uncertain about our own safety.

However, another fear is deeply entrenched in our thought processes, shaping our self-perceptions and relationships with one another. This fear pervades the human condition and increasingly permeates our world today: the fear of being seen as we really are. As author and therapist K. J. Ramsey writes, "The scariest part about being human might be those moments of exposure, when others see how deeply we need to be held."[5] We fear what would happen if others saw past our smiles into the truth of our pain and vulnerability. Anxiety is always about a felt sense of catastrophic aloneness and isolation.

Our world ruthlessly seeks to eliminate any opportunity for exposure: through glittering highlight reels and a constant influx of information, telling us who we need to be and how we need to act in order to be accepted. Voices, opinions, and assumptions flood our society, radiating with noise our bodies aren't biologically wired to handle and fueling the illusion that our worth is defined by what people say or do to us—perpetuating the belief that our value rests in what we have and what we do. And causing us to believe the lie that all those voices and assumptions fighting for our attention have a definitive say in who we are.

We can be caught in the shame-spiraling tension of our flaws and felt insufficiencies versus our picture-perfect perceptions of others. We constantly attempt to evolve into people we want or think we need to be. These factors only heighten our sense of anxiety, pulling us deeper into a false version of reality and away from the truth. We can experience people paralysis.

That synthetic smile stayed on my face, like a caked-on cosmetic, to the last day of my gap year and into the next four years of college. Although weeks of residential counseling had helped me feel less detached from my body, that sense of separation quickly relocated to a detachment from my experiences. I distanced myself from the agony of the last few years, refusing to confide in anyone about my struggles. I smiled so often and fiercely that people joked I never *stopped* smiling. If only they knew. I wasn't smiling on the inside. Down deep, I was terrified of rejection.

> I was terrified to be seen for who I thought I was,
> which was deeply intertwined and interpreted
> through the pain and shame in my story.

When the word *rejection* is peeled back to its Latin root, the term means "to throw back."[6] At the core of my anxiety, I deeply feared being "thrown back" by others. I feared what would happen if they saw the fetal-positioned, white-knuckled, recovering-anorexic, anxiety-riddled me. I envisioned others stepping back and disengaging, with glazed eyes and a gaze of cool judgment.

The fear of rejection pulsates throughout our generation. This fear runs so deep that it throws us into protecting ourselves from even the potential of experiencing it. We "throw ourselves back" before anyone else can by self-rejecting or isolating. We hide and pretend, giving others no opportunity to discount us, especially in our most vulnerable areas. Fear of rejection can often make us think in terms of scarcity. Keenly aware of our smallness and inner sense of not enoughness, we valiantly attempt to prove our worth externally. We can detach ourselves from our experiences of pain, wounding, and suffering and obsess with our external personas, desperate to convince others we deserve their acceptance and love.

Unable to control our acceptance or rejection by others, we frantically defend what we *can control.* We monitor our reputations. We manage our image. We stay guarded. We wear masks. We vigilantly cover our bases by casting blame and always attempting to prove ourselves right. We pretend we don't care. We people-please. We create distance between ourselves and those close to us, especially on difficult days. We smile away our pain like I did. We make sure all the parts we don't like about ourselves remain unseen.

Over and over again, I've seen my own scarcity mind-set create perceived enemies. My fear of rejection can often dehumanize others, twisting my perception of my relationships into sources of comparison and competition. Rather than seeing another person, I view others as threats to my own self-confidence and security.

On a recent trip to Israel, our study group and Jewish tour guide bussed to the border of Lebanon and Syria. Our end destination was an Israeli base nestled in the Golan Heights, where we would learn more about the past conflict between Israel and her neighboring countries. As we drove through winding mountain roads, we stopped unexpectedly.

"Out of the bus!" our tour guide announced. "And look to your right as you exit the vehicle!"

Our study group piled outside, meandering over to a thick concrete slab in the ground. Graffiti covered this oddly shaped and decades-old block that seemed to extend well beyond sight into the rocky earth.

"What is it?" someone asked once we had all gathered.

Our tour guide motioned us over to a hole in the ground, and as I peered down this darkened opening, I began to recognize the murky outline of a rusty stairwell.

"This is an old Syrian bunker, used by soldiers during the Six-Day War."

Surprise rippled through the group as we took turns climbing down these old steps into the center of the bunker, which snaked out like the slithering arms of an octopus with many different entrances and exits. When my turn came, I slowly descended into this black hole, clutching my iPhone with the flashlight turned on. The passageways leading to the bunker's protective chamber were incredibly narrow, and I had to force my way forward, shoulders rubbing concrete on both sides. Suddenly, I tripped and dropped my phone. Anxiety immediately gripped me. I was alone, in the dark. And I didn't know the way out.

I felt along the ground and quickly retrieved my phone, but not before I felt a sharp pang of recognition. I knew this feeling. The sickening wave of nausea. That sense of helpless isolation. That feeling of suffocating darkness closing like a tight fist around my lungs.

Fear can keep us locked in a metaphorical bunker, similar to this one. If anyone gets too close, we panic, gossip, bully, brag, or criticize. We do whatever it takes to regain our temporary sense of security. Fearing rejection if we are seen for who we think we are, we self-protect from being fully seen and known. However, our self-protection simultaneously keeps us from ever experiencing love or acceptance that goes deeper than the masks we wear. In a world that loves picture-perfect and hates failure, no one feels safe to come out. To risk exposure. However, as theologian Henri Nouwen explains, the "bombs" we build to maintain our sense of security and defend ourselves from our "enemies" are self-destructive in nature. Soon, we begin to realize that our security concerns are making us all dead before the bombs have exploded. They make us stiff and rigid.[7]

In the darkest days of my struggles with anxiety and anorexia, I envisioned God as absent from my pain and distant from my reach. But I've learned this is not the true God. The true God was in the bunker with me. And with you. He's closer than we think. If we crane our necks in search of him, he beckons us to go lower, not higher. That's where we'll find him.

The invitation he extends is to travel deeper into the darkness to find the Light. Rather than slamming our fists against the wall, trying to break down an exit, we have to turn further inside ourselves to discover the pathway to healing. Ironically, the gentle call of Jesus is to accept how broken we actually are. That's the first step toward changing. Only when we accept that we aren't fine and face reality can we begin our journey toward healing.

CHAPTER THREE

The Voice in My Head

On the bathroom floor that day in Germany, a light had switched off in the tender places of my soul, leaving me feeling stranded and alone in an echoing sense of my own vacancy. It was as if my capacity to live, to engage in life, had walked out and locked the door. My body felt like a numb shell, encasing a black expanse of nothingness. No joy, no pain. No emotion at all. Just numbness. But in the months following, I quickly discovered that the hollow state in which I found myself was anything but quiet.

How could you have fallen so far? Look at what you've done. You should be ashamed of yourself. The thoughts spilled from within, constantly pulling me into a spiral of self-loathing and shame. I wore insecurity like a blanket, an internal dialogue of self-criticism and fear becoming the soundtrack to my life. With a forceful energy that compelled me deeper into self-protection and hiding, my shame constantly told me a narrative that I was bad, that there was no hope for healing, and that I was utterly alone.

If mental health can be defined as a dedication to reality at all costs, then the kingdom of darkness is actively at work to keep us entangled in a skewed version of it. Anxiety often feels like we're living in chaos. We can't see anything correctly, as our vision becomes blinded with the terrifying imagery of what-ifs, worst-case scenarios, and a nerve-rattling sense of uncertainty. The Enemy breathes fear into us, intent on cementing this kind of thinking into our core operating system for navigating life. He is powerfully invested in these places of our deepest wounds and weaknesses, flooding our minds with a fogginess that is thickly misted with lies.

During my last few months in Germany, I took long walks around the Bodensee. During these shoreline laps, my surface-level smile concealed tangled knots of soul-deep wrestling. While my heart ached to be free, my head told me that self-protection was much safer.

> The kingdom of darkness is intent on attacking our minds, casting us as victims of our own vicious thought cycles and keeping us locked in the black pit of isolation.

The apostle John describes the Enemy as a murderer from the origins of time, never standing for truth, and full of nothing but lies. He is scripturally portrayed as a master of deception and the father of lies who speaks falsehoods as his native language (John 8:44 TPT). Directly opposing the purposes of God, the Enemy acts with characteristic hostility and aggression, yanking us into hiding over healing. He much prefers idealized personas over imperfect progress and fiercely promotes self-protection.

He plays into our discomfort and fear of being seen as we really are, causing us to question the safety of expressing the honest and painful truth of our experiences. He attempts to twist our perceptions of God and ourselves, flooding us with uncertainty about our ability to reach for healing. He seeks to distort our understanding of the stories we are living and our view of what is good, safe, and true. He tells us that expressing weakness, naming wounds, and being honest about our sin will only further isolate us instead of instilling hope within us.

You don't want to get hurt, do you?

Vulnerability is too risky.

You are safe here.

You are a burden to others.

The world is a scary place.

People are unpredictable.

You don't matter to anyone.

You better keep your guard up.

No one really cares.

What would others think?

On those long walks around the Bodensee, the Enemy caused me to question if life was worth living, if freedom is what I wanted, and if Jesus could be trusted. He reminded me often that this pit of isolation was familiar. Comfortable. All that I'd known. Against the voices and image-focused values of our world, darkness offered concealment for the version of myself that I was terrified of exposing.

The Enemy is actively at work to prevent us from even starting this inward journey. He will do everything to make us give up, give in, and lose hope. Sometimes he will triumphantly succeed. I know from personal experience: he's adept at attacking our most vulnerable places and then turning our failures against us. He doesn't want us to believe healing is possible and will do anything to make us doubt God's presence, goodness, and love.

The Enemy is strategic and cunning, acting stealthily to fill our minds with seething internal messages and deafening static in an attempt to distract and repel us from the truth. Recognizing that insecurity increases our susceptibly to his schemes, he tries to convince us to remain silent, stay small, and fold into despair. He often deceives us into believing God is distant and the Enemy is undefeatable. But the Enemy is predictable, and *we can actually decipher his patterns.* We can learn how to recognize them. He can attack us with a variety of methods. One prominent method is self-condemnation, also known as self-hatred.

The apostle Peter tells us the devil is incessantly roaming throughout the world, looking for prey to devour (1 Pet. 5:8 TPT). However, many of us underestimate the Enemy's hatred for us. He detests us and makes it one of his primary missions to get us to hate ourselves, too. Shredding our dignity and fixedly intent on our destruction, his most powerful work is often accomplished through his intrusion into our minds via our thought patterns. He knows if he can infiltrate our thoughts, he can control the direction of our lives.

For as long as I can remember, I've struggled with a relentless inner critic. My inner critic likes to live in the world of absolutes. Good or bad. Always or never. Everything is categorized in terms of black or white, with little room for nuance or gray. Without question, my inner critic's favorite word is "should." This nagging voice in the back of my head delights in reminding me of how insecure, different, and defective I am.

My inner critic rarely allows me to just *enjoy* a social gathering or conversation. Afterward, I often feel like I'm on trial. Defenseless against a ruthless interrogator who picks apart every word I said. More often than not, this internal hot seat leaves me in a haze of self-judgment and regret over the smallest perceived error.

Regardless of what went wrong and who was involved, my inner critic tells me I'm at fault. I'm the one who messed up. I am bad. I must take the blame. This unrelenting voice rants a daily cacophony of self-abuse: overanalyzing, pounding, judging, blaming, criticizing, accusing, catastrophizing, and second-guessing.[1]

Some days, I want to crawl out of my head. No matter how hard I try, I can't seem to escape this loop of negative self-talk.

> How am I supposed to interrupt a
> conversation between me and . . . me?

Most people have attributed my inner critic to my perfectionist personality type. But to some degree, don't we all battle with a berating voice in our heads? No one is fully exempt. We call this voice many different names: Our inner critic. Negative self-talk. Self-criticism. The longer I walk this inward journey, the less I see my inner critic as an unfortunate character trait and more as an intentional tool the Enemy employs in the battle for my mind.

The voices of darkness can flood us from a host of different sources: societal messages, childhood experiences, and wounds inflicted by others. But the Enemy is not only scheming and strategic; he's also subtle. One of his schemes is to slip into the narrative of your mind and disguise himself as you. Rather than speaking audibly to us, he slips into our thoughts, causing us to believe his voice of self-condemnation originated from us. That is his method of deception. The thoughts intruding on us come in such a personal singular way that we mistakenly believe they are our thoughts. The Enemy seeks to make his voice so pervasive that we can't differentiate his voice from our own:

You will never measure up.

You're a failure.

You're not enough.

You're such a hypocrite.

You're disgusting.

No one will ever love you.

You're stupid.

You deserve to be alone.

You're so dumb.

You've blown it again.

Personalizing his criticism of our loudest insecurities and deepest wounds, the Enemy barrages us with negative "self-talk." As we become entangled in his accusations, we begin to construct monstrous self-perceptions. Negative self-perceptions fuel vicious self-contempt and, eventually, we can hardly stand to be with *ourselves*. As we search for an escape from our own self-loathing, the Enemy urges us to self-destruct.

> The Enemy has achieved his ultimate goal
> when we begin to do his work for him.

During my remaining months in Germany, I grew so accustomed to the overwhelming intensity of my inner critic that I couldn't imagine anything different. I progressively withdrew from social settings, collapsing further inside myself and wearing a happy expression almost subconsciously. One person, however, saw past my frozen smile into lacerating self-loathing. After dinner one evening in February, the director of my Bible college (we'll call him S) asked to speak with me. Knowing that *he knew* about my doctor's appointment and diagnosis, I questioned my ability to walk into the room, let alone look him in the face.

Capitalizing on the evening's icy weather, I layered on knitted sweaters and wrapped my arms tightly around my shoulders like protective shields—anything to create a buffer against the raw feeling of exposure. When I walked into S's office and took the chair that he offered, my shoulders stayed curled and eyes lowered. Bundled in wool up to my neckline, I sat rigidly on the edge of my seat, waiting for a string of well-justified questions sprinkled with subtle rebuke. But he didn't say anything. Not one word. Eventually, I glanced up, my eyes connecting with his.

He was watching me through kind, fatherly eyes.

When he began to speak, his tone was gentle: "I've seen hundreds of students complete this program," he momentarily stared past me as if he was watching invisible images of old memories flicker across the wall. "They come from a variety of backgrounds. But most, if not all of them, have one thing in common: they are all trying to leave something in their past. They come here to learn about the Bible, hoping that theological head knowledge will deconstruct their pain so they can attempt to rebuild their lives. But pain rarely works that way. Neither does God. He draws many students here, not so they can forget about their pain *but face it.*"

S leaned forward. "You've been on my mind, Taylor. Even before I heard about your doctor's appointment and diagnosis, I've been praying for you."

I stared at him, mind reeling at the warmth with which he engaged me. The grace sitting at the core of our conversation seeped inward, disorienting my sense of shame.

After a brief pause, he continued. "Over the last few days, my wife and I have been listening to a song. Would you mind if I played it for you?"

At my quick affirmative nod, he turned toward his laptop, "It's called 'Be Kind to Yourself.'" As the voice of Andrew Peterson flooded the room, his eyes filled with tears even before mine did. We silently cried together as the lyrics played. The song painted a picture of someone feeling as if they're drowning in self-loathing, the threads in their voice testifying to their longing to escape themselves. To be someone else. Anyone else. I resonated with every word. "Be kind to yourself," Peterson gently sang, even when your self-directed anger and self-destructive thoughts scream the opposite. Something inside me snapped as I continued to listen to him describe a never-ending internal battle between you and you. How does it ever end? This was my question as well. The next phrase of the song rattled me. "Gotta learn to love, learn to love, learn to love your enemies too." [2]

As the song ended, my mind drifted back to my doctor's appointment with G. The whole ordeal had been excruciating, but one part especially had caused me to inwardly writhe. Toward the beginning of the appointment, I met briefly with a primary care physician. Not a specialist in eating disorders, this female doctor had been less than understanding. As I haltingly explained my symptoms, the director's wife translating my answers into German, she stared at me with a cool and accusing gaze. She didn't invite me to share my history. She didn't extend her hand for a handshake. Her expression reflected the cold, white walls of her office, an empty canvas for my silent and unacknowledged shame. As she listened to my self-destructive tendencies, everything about her tone and mannerisms exuded suspicion and screamed *your fault*.

I messed up.

I was the one to blame.

As I sat in S's office and remembered her blonde hair and blue eyes, I envisioned my own similar features and realized how much she reminded me of me. She looked at me the way I looked at myself. As my mind worked to piece together fragmented thoughts, a realization ripped through me. Despite all my frantic attempts at self-protection, was I my own worst enemy?

There was no way to escape *me*.

The feeling of being trapped inside my own body had become so intense that I'd eventually reverted to self-destruction. Consumed with self-hatred, I was blinded to the forces of evil around me. Our actual Enemy, the devil, knows that his most powerful and destructive work can be accomplished when we don't believe in his existence. As long as we don't wonder about his presence, he can do whatever he wants without us even recognizing his attack. Evil will do anything to prevent us from inviting God into our anxiety and experiences of pain. He attempts to shift the blame to others. Our friends. Our family. And best of all? Ourselves.[3]

I left S's office exhausted and feeling battered by the unspoken thoughts flooding my mind. The grace that S had extended to me lingered with a soft rush of awareness, as if the glow of a flickering candle held light against my inner hollowness. As I crawled into bed, hands and feet icy, my gaze drifted to the ceiling. I listened to the dark and spiraling chaos of my mind. Where were all these condemning thoughts coming from? A loving God? I didn't think so.

CHAPTER FOUR

But How Do I Even Get through Today?

There's a promise in the Bible that I've often doubted is true for me. While teaching in the bustling temple courts of Jerusalem, Jesus is recorded as proclaiming the following line when speaking of the new life purchased for us through his imminent crucifixion and resurrection: "If the Son sets you free, you will be free indeed" (John 8:36 NIV).

What? Really? When I was a little girl, I prayed a prayer confessing my sin and surrendering my life to Jesus. I understood the gospel and genuinely believed it. The Son had set me free! I was told that angels were rejoicing in heaven, my name was written in the Book of Life, and I would spend eternity with Jesus. I fell asleep that night feeling new and confident and hopeful. I believed he loved me and was pleased with me, and I was going to live the life that he intended.

Over the next decade, my confidence slowly faded as I realized my prayer hadn't fixed my pain, shame, and struggles. In fact, I seemed to struggle more after that day. During my gap year in

Germany, I'd collided with the shattering uncertainty that perhaps this promise wasn't applicable to me. I didn't feel free. In the Gospel of John, Jesus says that although the Enemy comes only to steal, kill, and destroy, he came so that we could have life, and have it in full (John 10:10 NIV). But the narrative I was carrying in my body told a different story than the triumphant one I'd learned to expect and esteem. My reality didn't match the glorious reality guaranteed to me in Scripture, which caused me to feel trapped inside my pain and outside God's grace. What does that verse even mean?

> I wasn't sure what to do with this promise of full life when I was just asking Jesus to help me get through today.

When the Enemy can't drown out Jesus's whispers, he'll cause us to doubt Jesus's words. Notice that I didn't say completely *stop* believing in Jesus's words, just a subtle doubting. I can believe that freedom is real for other people. But when I envision him speaking to *me,* leaned in, face close to mine, whispering these words about that one wound. That one scar. That one struggle. That one hurt. That one lie I just can't seem to unbelieve. That one thing, while I'm feeling like a failure? I doubt him. Maybe freedom for others, but certainly not for me.

Does God even see me? Does God love me? Does God care? Does God have a purpose for me? Is his Word true for my life? Is that kind of freedom accessible to me? The pain and suffering etched into our stories can morph into silent shame, gnawing at our souls and twisting our perception of how attainable this promised freedom is for us. Am I the only one? Especially in areas of relentless struggle and stinging despair, we'll experience Satan's second prominent strategy in preventing us from moving forward: self-deception.

Self-deception is defined as "the action or practice of allowing oneself to believe that a false or unvalidated feeling, idea, or situation is true."[1] Every destructive weapon and evil force in the Enemy's dominion is set on deceiving us into believing we are forever stuck in our self-loathing, scars, and shame. He wants us to believe that our wounds run deeper than love, that our sin drives us beyond the outskirts of grace, and that our struggles disqualify us from the steadfastness of God's presence.

Over years of piled-up evidence that seems to validate these assumptions, our vision becomes clouded with a cheap version of the gospel that seems to align better with our current reality. The shame screeching into our lives causes us to question our willpower to walk through *today*, let alone find the grit to keep on hoping when our pain isn't lessening. The Enemy floods us with septic infusions of uncertainty and singles us out as the one exception to Jesus's promise.

He doesn't really mean you.

You're a hopeless case.

You're too far gone.

You're a disappointment.

Your situation is beyond repair.

You're damaged goods.

Why even try?

His primary lie: there is no way out. Maybe for other people. But not for you. Over the last few years, the hardest part about this inward journey hasn't necessarily been walking it, but believing that with Jesus I can.

A well-known Thai story describes a man who was passing a herd of elephants when he stopped, confused. As he moved closer, he noticed that the elephants were all being held by a small rope tied to their front leg. No chains. No cage. They just stood still, making no attempt to escape. Walking up to a trainer nearby, the man asked why these elephants stayed bound when they clearly had the ability to break free.

The trainer responded quickly, "When the elephants are very young and much smaller, their trainers use a similar size rope to tie them. At that age, it's enough to hold them. As they grow up, they are conditioned to believe they can't break free. They believe the rope can still hold them, so they never try to escape. Even though they are strong enough to break the rope, they believe they can't, so they feel trapped right where they are." The man left, deep in thought. Those elephants had the ability to break free from their bonds, but they believed they couldn't. So they never tried.

> As I've untangled all the factors that brought me to this crisis point, one factor is indisputably my own belief that freedom simply wasn't possible.

I was too sick. Too broken. Healing was hopelessly out of reach for me. I draped the shame of my experiences over myself and God, dissatisfied with the life I was living and the body I was inhabiting. My faith, which had initially been the hope to which I clung, became a cause of disappointment. I didn't realize then that shame was what the Enemy was leveraging to keep me stuck. Right there, in all my despair and emptiness and unraveling. In this place of isolation, he'd conditioned my mind to believe that lonely endurance was my new reality. I was stuck. I could never be free.

Many of us have experienced a similar kind of Enemy conditioning. We start our new lives with Jesus with unswerving hope, exuberant joy, and full confidence: *the Son has set me free*! But slowly, those air-sucking waves of anxiety hijack our confidence. Old struggles persist under the surface of our lives, and disruptive thoughts slink into the corners of our minds. Past wounds continue to throb, still shaping our relationships and responses in life. We realize, with a pang of disappointment, that the promise of eternal life doesn't necessarily mean an *easy life*. We grapple with the daily undoing of what we hoped life would be today.

Pain and poor decisions and unforeseen problems and previous regrets plague us, throwing shadows on our present joy. Soon, we fight to hold on to hope. The Enemy is at work, knotting ropes in darkened corners of our mind. Then, there comes a moment when we break. We feel shattered into an unfixable pile of pieces. We fail, or someone fails us. Deep down, we feel like maybe God failed us. We come to the edge of ourselves, wrestling with the tension of the life we are living against the full life promised to us in Christ. We don't feel free.

On that day, we decide it hurts too much to hope.

So we agree with the Enemy: *Yes, I'm stuck. You're right. I will never be free.* We sink into numbness. Settle into the belief that a different kind of life is impossible. His lies become so deeply entrenched in our mind-sets that we withdraw those tender parts of our hearts from the hands of Jesus, finding him only on the fringes of our lives.

God's promises, once fresh and vibrant, feel stale and inauthentic in comparison to the undeniable tenderness of childhood wounds. The deep scars of abuse. And the potent strength of addiction, eating disorders, poisonous comparison, broken promises, sexual sin, feelings of worthlessness, suicidal thoughts, anxiety, and depression. The ropes of shame, defeat, and isolation that the Enemy knots into our stories are painfully present, chafing and scraping at our souls. But in the rawness of their reality in our lives, matched with our own human powerlessness, we can forget they are not more powerful than the cross.

When Jesus sacrificed his life and rose again three days later, he didn't just assure us future spots in heaven and abandon us to our best efforts today. He defeated the Enemy by becoming sin and bondage for us (2 Cor. 5:21 NIV), disabling his present power over our lives. What does this mean? The snares of self-deception no longer have to entangle us. No matter what the Enemy says to us or about us, *we are not trapped.*

I'm learning that Jesus's declaration of freedom over me and my envisioning of freedom's outworking in my life are two very different things. While I visualize glossy images of instantaneous healing and a sparkly before-and-after story, Jesus invites me to bring my lingering pain and unfixed struggles to him as he tells a bigger story with my life than I can see. In this story, the cross declares the following victorious truth over each of our lives: regardless of who we are or where we find ourselves, we are not helplessly stuck.

We are not alone. We are not abandoned. We are never forgotten.

We are also not called to live in shame. The Enemy often tells us that our role is to carry the resulting shame of the pain and struggles in our experiences. In spiritual environments that tend to elevate the stories of overcomers and ostracize the struggles of the wounded, our feelings of shame can simply be compounded. But we are not called to live in shame. Jesus's sacrificial death permanently removed our shame so we don't have to carry it anymore. He promises to heal the wounds of the brokenhearted, proclaim freedom for the captives, make beauty from ashes, strengthen those crushed by despair, and redeem the darkest parts of our stories (Isa. 61:1–3 TPT). That is the story of the cross. But more often than not, I feel like I need to hold my shame as my own punishment.

My battles with anorexia and anxiety have repeatedly persuaded me away from living in that truth. Despair and frustration can drag me into a dark canyon of doubt, especially when I'm in the middle of a still-messy story with no tangible end in sight. Hope dwindles in the space between what we thought life was going to be and what life really is. This inward journey requires diligence and is rarely linear. Never perfect.

> Hope reawakens when I begin to view Jesus's declaration of freedom over me not as a quick fix to all my messes but as an invitation to the relational reconditioning of my mind.

When the Israelite nation was released from captivity in Egypt, they became instantly free. Absolutely, totally, 100 percent free. Although they were free the minute they stepped foot out of Egypt, one glance at the book of Exodus reveals they *certainly didn't act free.*

They had wounds from their past.

They had struggles in their present.

They had fears about their future.

An entire Old Testament book records the Israelite nation cyclically grumbling, complaining, doubting God, wounding each other, and sabatoging themselves. Again and again and again. For four hundred years, the Israelite nation had been conditioned by their slave drivers to believe that freedom would never be a possible reality for them. When God redeemed them from captivity, the Israelites' visible bondage had been removed, but not the invisible and even deeper chains of self-deception. For the next forty years, they journeyed through the desert as God healed their hearts and reconditioned their minds from a slave mentality to a son-and-daughter mentality. The Israelites' journey after leaving Egypt represents the inward journey that we must take every day.

Thousands of years later, Paul wrote about God's ultimate rescue in his letter to the church of Colossae: "He has rescued us completely from the tyrannical rule of darkness and has translated us into the kingdom realm of his beloved Son. For in the Son all our sins are canceled and we have the release of redemption *through his very blood*" (Col. 1:13–14 TPT—emphasis in original).

When God saved us, we were instantly set free. Absolutely, totally, 100 percent free. Just like the Israelites, however, we don't immediately begin acting free. We, too, have wounds from our past, struggles in the present, and fears about the future. Over the course of our lives, God longs to heal our shame and recondition our minds from a slave mentality to a son-and-daughter mentality. He will always be walking with us into deeper levels of restoration and freedom, in different areas and in different ways.

What does this mean for you and me today? I've often chalked up this inward journey to a litany of emotional breakthroughs and life-altering moments where I've felt a marked shift toward healing. But I'm learning that the call of Jesus is much more ordinary, inviting me into the weeds of my daily experience. Rather than a dramatic journey, Jesus calls me into smaller, simpler, and more concrete actions. What is that next step in front of me? I don't have to know the big steps to take the little steps. And I only have to take one step at a time. The Israelites' journey teaches us that when we strain our eyes too far ahead, discouragement seeps in. I've continually had to remind myself to lower my gaze and commit to taking the small step in front of me. Today, focus on taking the next step. Do the next right thing. Make the next right choice. Take the next step with Jesus.

- Reach out to your friend.
- Send the text.
- Make the phone call.
- Say "I need help" to someone you trust.
- Verbalize the wound.
- Expose the lie.
- Delete Instagram.

- Lock up your laptop.
- Confess what really happened.
- Reveal your unforgiveness.
- Be honest with yourself.
- Own your mistake.
- Extend grace to yourself.
- Allow yourself to feel the pain.
- Give yourself permission to cry.

Freedom is found not so much in those glorious, emotional moments but in these consistent forward steps during daily life. When we look back, we'll see a long journey of little steps. Not self-improvement steps or self-help steps, but Jesus steps.

I wrestled with telling my parents the truth about the extent of my struggles with anxiety and anorexia. G had asked eighteen-year-old me to inform them for liability reasons, but a deeper part of me ached for them to know. One evening, I sat on the floor in the narrow hallway outside of my room: back leaning against the wall, legs crisscrossed, laptop opened. My international phone plan didn't include texting, so email was the next best option. (I'd already concluded I wasn't brave enough to tell them over the phone!)

Logging into my email, I stared at my blank screen, cursor blinking, for a long time. I typed slowly as my heart formed words, one sentence at a time. Unsure of what to write in the subject line, I typed "prayer request." After one last moment of hesitancy, I pressed send. I didn't realize it then, but I'd just taken my next small step with Jesus.

CHAPTER FIVE

An Invitation to the Sacred Place

When my mom replied to my email about the truth of my struggles with anxiety and anorexia, I didn't open it right away. I stared at her unopened response, heat flushing my body as I wrestled to harness a host of untethered emotions. For the first time in years, I'd tiptoed out of my inner darkness into the light of honesty. How would she respond?

After a few moments of faltering indecision, I clicked open the email.

As I read, heart soaking in one paragraph at a time, her words dismantled my defenses and diffused grace into wounds I didn't realize I had. Hesitantly, my tense muscles released and welcomed relief. Her words spoke solace and pledged companionship, as if she was reaching through my screen and taking up the space next to me, promising to shoulder this burden with me. The journey ahead was no longer *mine* but *ours*. I read the following paragraph over and over and over again.

I will continue to run to the Throne for you and with you. We are both so very capable that sometimes we trick ourselves into believing that WE can do whatever needs to be done—even without God. In his love and mercy, he allows us to experience things we can't control or conquer. He wants us to surrender to self-reliance and self-dependency. In these battles, we must go to the Throne utterly defeated and acknowledge that *he* is *Lord*. This is the outworking of *he* is the vine and we are the branches. Apart from him, we can do nothing. We just don't believe it sometimes! I will pray for hope for you. I will pray that you will see *God* and not the problem.

Have you ever been in a stressful or intense situation, and once it's resolved you sink into a chair and suddenly realize how exhausted you actually are? The moment my honesty brushed shoulders with compassion, years of pent-up adrenaline slowly drained from me. I was exhausted . . . and not just physically, but emotionally. In that moment, I felt utterly defeated. However, over the next few years, I wrestled with the latter half of my mom's message.

Was I willing to acknowledge that *he* is *Lord*?

As I've walked this healing journey, there's been a point of constant contention between me and God. I've wanted to determine what steps I take, when I take them, how I take them, and where they lead me. I've ached for freedom, but I've also wanted to get there my own way. On my own terms.

> My criteria: no pain, fastest route, fewest life alterations possible.

Defeat was easy to acknowledge; letting go of self-reliance and self-dependence was far more difficult to accept. The steps forward I envisioned for myself smelled of self-help. Self-help focuses on me, submits to my emotional whims, and stays within the bounds of my perceived control. This is why self-help typically results only in temporary freedom. The extent of my healing stays surface level and is limited to the faulty confines of self-effort.

Most of us aren't looking for temporary freedom but long-term transformational freedom. This kind of freedom can only be encountered when taking Jesus steps, not self-help steps. And Jesus steps can't be taken without . . . well . . . *Jesus*.

My emotional whims must submit to Jesus, and my sense of control must bow to him. My will must be broken and surrendered to his will, my steps tracing the path that he has set for me. British evangelist Roy Hession described this surrender: "It is being 'Not *I*, but Christ,' . . . and a 'C' is a bent 'I.'"[1]

When my mom and I talked on the phone a few hours later, I tentatively brought up the possibility of counseling once I started my freshman year of college that fall.

After a pause, my mom replied softly, "Your dad and I are looking into residential treatment programs for this summer."

My vision blurred as I comprehended the implications of her words. I balked immediately. No. A big no. That would *not* be the story of my life. I was willing to do counseling. Not treatment. When I responded, I heard the threads of panic in my voice, "But, I don't want *that*. But, I don't think I need *that* . . ."

Despite my sense of defeat, I was afraid and still fiercely grasped control over my story. Treatment would place my recovery completely in the hands of others, and I wanted to determine my own steps forward. I didn't want to take Jesus steps, which would require the surrender of my story to him. The call with my parents lasted for an hour and included many *But, Is*. Only toward the end of the conversation did I begin to bend to Jesus.

The following day, along with a few links to residential treatment program websites, my mom sent me these prophetic words from the book of Isaiah:

> See, I am doing a new thing!
>> Now it springs up; do you not perceive it?
> I am making a way in the wilderness
>> and streams in the wasteland. . . .
> I provide water in the wilderness
>> and streams in the wasteland,
> to give drink to my people, my chosen,
>> the people I formed for myself
>> that they may proclaim my praise. (Isa. 43:19–21 NIV)

When the Israelite nation left Egypt and began their journey to Canaan, God could have guided them on a more direct and much easier route. The fastest route between the two places?

Eleven days.

But in his sovereignty, he didn't set them on the eleven-day path. He chose to guide them on an unconventional, circuitous path through desert spaces. Although their rebellion lengthened the trip significantly, God intentionally launched them on a course that seemed illogical, painful, and meandering to the human eye. Of course, they fought against him.

Why this way? They protested. *Do you see us? Do you care about us? Do you know what you're doing? Are you truly in control?*

God's response? Yes, yes, yes, and yes . . . but he had different priorities than the Israelites did. He cared more about their connection with him than their comfort. He saw into the future and knew that the fast and easy route wouldn't result in long-term freedom. They'd rely on themselves and eventually sabotage their own efforts. They would stand in the way of their own healing process. He knew the Israelites had to reach the end of themselves, releasing their perceived sense of control completely, to encounter the person who could free them internally. The new thing he was doing among them could only be encountered on the wilderness route.

> Like the Israelites, I often want the new thing God is doing in my life without the wilderness experience.

As an eighteen-year-old facing a long and lonely summer in residential treatment, I angrily questioned, Why this way? I doubted God's wisdom, love, and care. If God had so much power, why couldn't he just heal me now? I wanted my life back. I wanted quick healing . . . on my time, in my own way. But God had different priorities than I did. As with the Israelites, he cared more about my connection with him than my comfort. He knew the fast and easy route wouldn't result in my long-term freedom. I needed an experience that would bring me to the end of myself. And that is a long journey.

While I begged God to give me what I wanted so I could believe he truly loved me, God loved me enough to give me what I needed so I could experience him more fully. And in my fuller experience of him, I would begin to experience the transformation my heart truly wanted.

In the wilderness, I met the real God and began to build my faith not on his good gifts but on the Giver of those gifts.

In the wilderness, God worked to root out the desolate, dry, and deadened places in me to create space for the flourishing of new life.

In the wilderness, God began the process of carving out the slave patterns in me, reconditioning my mind, and teaching me how to live like a daughter.

My summer in residential treatment was long, arduous, and incredibly painful. I learned that, rather than our best efforts, God often chooses our broken wills as the birthing place for new things. Why? As my will was broken, this inward journey became less about me (what I want) and more about God ("I am yours").

Pain shifted my perspective from the hard thing in front of me to his presence with me. The journey became less about the route and more about our relationship. Since that point, every moment that I've chosen to bend to Jesus and say "I trust you," and then act on that trust, I have encountered more of the new thing he is doing in my life.

This wilderness experience takes two different forms in Scripture: deep waters and desert places. These locations are the primary places for God's transformative work in the lives of biblical characters.

- In deep waters, the Israelites turned from panicked captives to praising children.
- In desert spaces, Elijah turned from powerless victim to prophetic voice.
- In desert spaces, Moses turned from grumbling fugitive to friend of God.
- In deep waters, Jonah turned from rebellious to repentant.
- In desert spaces, Hagar turned from helpless to heard by God.
- In desert spaces, Joseph turned from accused to appointed.
- In desert spaces, Abraham turned from father of none to father of many.
- In deep waters, Noah turned from outcast to "one who walked with God."
- In desert spaces, David turned from shepherding herds to shepherding hearts.

- In desert spaces, Job turned from testing God to trusting God.
- In desert spaces, Abigail turned from abused wife to wise advocate.
- In deep waters, the disciples turned from fear to faith.
- In desert spaces, Deborah turned from lowly woman to leader of warriors.

Even Jesus was not exempt from a wilderness experience. Jesus himself was *sent* into the desert *by the Spirit* (Mark 1:12). During every painful moment of his earthly experience, he bent his will to the Father, no matter the circumstances or cost. In the garden of Gethsemane, our redemption was won not by Peter's fierce fighting but by Jesus's broken whisper, "Not my will, but your will be done." As he later modeled on the cross, transformational freedom cannot occur without pain and sacrifice.

What if the place you don't want to go . . . physically, emotionally, relationally . . . is the place where God wants to begin the new thing in you? How often do we fight against God as he draws us into a wilderness experience where we'll meet him most profoundly? As we kick and scream and drag our feet, he's patiently waiting for us to trust him. Trust that his ways are truly best.

> "I'm so scared, I'm so scared, I'm so scared . . ."

This mantra ran repetitively through my mind as my dad pulled up to a residential treatment facility located in the grassy hills of Indiana. My admittance had been scheduled for mid-April. I'd finished my gap year in Germany only two weeks earlier.

The past fourteen days had been a dizzying whirlwind of packing, catching flights, unpacking, repacking, and catching more flights. I'd survived but was a vacant shell, physically present and emotionally absent. Numbed out. Detached from reality. Consumed with anxiety. Hanging on to hope by frayed threads. During our few days together, time stood still for both me and my parents, whose pain exceeded even my own. We cried together as they affirmed their love and support.

My dad and I drove to the treatment facility together. When we arrived, he hoisted my suitcase from the trunk and we walked into the building side by side. My treatment team introduced themselves and gave him a brief tour of the large, ranch-style home where I would be staying for the next two and a half months. Then, leaving us in a small waiting room, they gave us a few moments to say goodbye.

As my dad prepared to leave, I clung to him, terrified. Tears filled his eyes as he bent down and kissed my forehead, "I love you, and I'm so proud of you."

I hiccuped sobs as he hugged me tightly and whispered a short prayer, "Father, I entrust Taylor into your loving arms now. . . ." Posture slumped as if he carried a crushing weight on his shoulders, he willed himself out the front entrance and gently shut the door.

I steeled myself for another sweeping wave of loneliness, but I never did feel alone. The gentle arms of my Heavenly Father encircled me and held me close. *You are safe here with me. I love you. I am for you. I will never let you go. You are mine.* As my tears continued to stream, my mind wandered to a memory from a few years ago.

Years ago, I heard a story about a family who had adopted several children. When the family's adoption was finalized, the case manager encouraged these newly adoptive parents to spend time swimming with their children.

"The pool forces physical contact," she explained, "which is often the quickest route to emotional connection. The children can't swim on their own, so they have to hold on to the adoptive parents in order to stay afloat."

These children had already experienced significant childhood trauma. Wanting to form healthy attachments quickly, the recently enlarged family spent almost every afternoon at the pool. Most of the children delighted in the affection and care of an adoptive family. Their less-wounded hearts allowed for quicker bonds of trust, and they almost immediately began calling their new parents Mommy and Daddy. At the pool, they clung to their parents with white-knuckled grips as they explored the deep end together, their nervous giggling eventually shifting into laughter and squeals of delight.

However, one of the children who had experienced the most trauma remained reticent. She wasn't sure about new pools or new parents. She had settled into calling her new parents a generic "the dad" and "the mom." She also refused to go into the deep end, eyes distrusting and heart wary.

One afternoon, however, while she played near the pool's shallow end, the ripples of a nearby splash caught her by surprise. Guard dropping in a moment of spiked anxiety, she lunged forward with a gasp, "*Mommy!*"

Her adoptive mother turned, eyes wide. The little girl's eyes widened too.

In this brief moment of emotional unguardedness, she allowed her mother to reach over and gently pull her close, encircling her into a tight embrace. They began drifting into the deep end together. The little girl didn't fight back. Head lowered and mouth inches from her ear, her adoptive mother began whispering words that were imperceptible to everyone but her: *You're safe here with me. I love you. I am for you. I will never let you go. You are mine.*

The little girl's stiff body, taunt from years of trauma, relaxed completely and she began to visibly melt into her adoptive mom's embrace. Years of hypervigilant, legitimate self-protection were—for a brief moment—rendered powerless against the overwhelming peace of strong arms.

This little girl's scary place had turned into a sacred space.

Four years later, on my first day of residential treatment, I felt my anxiety slowly melt into heavenly arms as I allowed God to gently guide me into my own version of deep waters. *Father*, my heart gasped. He was not just *the* Father, but *my* Father. When I released control and rested against him, he pulled me close and told me he was with me and would never let me go. He turned my scary place into a sacred space too.

I recently read an article that identified the defining characteristics of sacred places throughout history and across religions:

- A focusing lens
- A place of communication with God
- A point of contact with God
- A locus of divine power that transforms and heals a human life
- A natural map that provides direction to life
- An orientation[2]

Deep waters and desert spaces are not the absence of God's love and mercy, but sacred spaces of intimacy, connection, healing, and communication. God becomes personal in these scary places.

When we turn to him, even for the briefest of moments, our Father enfolds us in his strong arms and speaks softly to us, whispering truths about who he is and who we are in him. Beth Guckenberger writes, "The exchange often ends up being less about the words and more about the message. The message sounds like, *I love you. I made you. I see you. I forgive you. I will use you. Come into my presence. Go out into the world.* It's a spiritual language, and we'll spend a lifetime becoming fluent in it."[3]

My scary place wasn't outside the bounds of God's care or control. Rather, he'd been already there, waiting for me, and welcoming me in. Over the next few weeks, as my breathing slowed and deepened, questions lingered: What would it look like to trust that God's way was best, even when his way looked far different from my own? What would it look like to trust that this hard thing in front of me was part of the good story God was writing with my life? I felt the shame and anxiety knotted in my spirit begin to unravel.

What if this wilderness route is where he'd wanted to meet me all along?

part two

CHAPTER SIX

Bleeding in a Thousand Places

Slowly, I began to see the many defense mechanisms I utilized to avoid connecting deeply with my fears, anxiety, and unhealed hurts. My self-protective tendencies not only kept others out but also kept me from becoming acquainted with the person who hid behind my *I'm fines* and happy smiles. I'd lost sight of who I was. The slave patterns entrenched in my thinking simmered beneath the surface of my awareness, causing me to feel unfree without understanding the deeper root. Part of this journey included identifying and untangling all the threads of my slave patterns sitting behind my thought cycles, my responses, and my reactions.

As I read about the Israelites' journey through their wilderness route in the book of Exodus, I began to understand that their journey wasn't just about reaching Canaan. Rather, this journey was one of God exposing them to themselves. Their trek through seemingly endless stretches of sand resounds with this deeper purpose of God. He continually gave them glimpses of the slave mentality embedded in their thinking, revealing to them the shame, fear, and inner bondage still embedded within.

This was the work of Love, fiercely intent on their healing and freedom.

God invited me into a similar process during the tail end of my time in residential treatment, but those first few weeks of therapy I was too exhausted and emotionally raw. My sense of defeat matched that of the prophet Elijah in 1 Kings 19. This chapter records Elijah sinking into a deep depression, consumed with fear after receiving death threats from a queen named Jezebel. After he entered into a wilderness journey with God, the prophet's knees weakened in despair, overwhelmed by a wave of resurfacing emotions that refused to be stuffed and silenced anymore.

"I have had enough, Lord," he cried.

I'm not enough for any of this. I'm not enough for the journey ahead. I'm not enough for this thing I'm facing. I'm not enough to survive this pain. I'm not enough to take even the next step. I'm not enough for my life.

The prophet Elijah begged God to just let him die. God's response?

Eat, drink, sleep.

". . . or the journey ahead will be too much for you" (1 Kings 19:7 NLT). God's whisper to the prophet Elijah soothed my own frayed soul. Desiring my stillness before him first, God slowed me to rhythms of rest that eventually calmed my internal frantic. Only when I sat, quieted before him, did God begin to expose the slave patterns *in me* in order to extract them *out of me.*

You see, no one intentionally chooses a slave mentality. Most of us slip into the mind-set slowly and then become progressively entangled in it. Similar to a trainer conditioning the mind of a baby elephant, the Enemy's conditioning of our minds is a slow and subtle process that is almost impossible to detect in the moment. By the time we sense we are stuck and *something feels deeply off* inside us, the opportunity to simply step away from the Enemy's conditioning is long past. Just like the Israelites after leaving Egypt, we become so ensnared in his lies that we aren't sure who we are apart from them.

When does the Enemy's mind-conditioning process begin? Typically, in our first experiences with the razor-sharp edges of pain. Maybe a callous remark? An absent parent? Abuse? Loss? Betrayal?

> As children, we are wounded when the inevitable brokenness in our world cuts at our hearts.

No one is exempt. Few of us know what to do. In the first years of life, how do you process the moment when your safety is stripped from you? How do you process when the person who is supposed to shield you from harm hurts you? How do you process the pain of loving someone that you never knew or will never see again? How do you process scarring, soul-shaping words when you haven't yet learned what's true? And what do you do when those same wounds keep getting picked at and dug into, making your heart bleed again and again? Who wouldn't reach for protective cover to prevent our vulnerable selves from being wounded again?

In our weakest moments, the Enemy urges us to avoid future vulnerability *at all costs*. He offers us ways to cope in our cruel world. He tells us we must hide. To stay safe, we heap on layers of falseness. To survive, we hide behind filters and fakeness. To prevent pain from unraveling us ever again, we evolve and adapt into inauthentic versions of ourselves. This is when . . .

- The people-pleaser learns to find approval in staying small and always saying yes.

- The performer learns to find acceptance in staying big and promoting a winsome image.
- The perfectionist learns that producing perfection leaves no margin for failure.
- The bully learns that demonstrating power dulls her own inner defenselessness.
- The manipulator learns to use words as a strategy against her own sense of helplessness.
- The achiever learns to measure her worth by nothing other than her success.
- The beauty queen learns to measure her worth by skin-deep standards only.
- The peacekeeper learns to stay safe by always conceding at the first sign of conflict.
- The conformer learns that blending in conceals insecurity and dulls self-doubt.
- The rebel learns that defiance gives no opportunity for betrayal or crushed hopes.
- The helper learns that "being needed" numbs her own need for affection and affirmation.
- The comedian learns to settle for the shallow love that lingers behind others' laughter.
- The gossip learns that picking apart other people pacifies her own picked-open heart.

These Enemy-induced coping patterns harden and hollow us, requiring us to slip behind masks and conform to actors' roles. We become adept at playing games and practicing a dance with darkness. So many of us are caught up in this dance, numb and asleep, our hearts vowing never to experience the hell of getting hurt again.

Over the years, however, these patterns deepen their grooves. Our protective layers, once purposeful (to alleviate pain), bind us and become permanent (our pattern for life). They dictate our decisions and determine how we operate and perceive our world. These protective layers and patterns of falseness, darkness, self-deception, and wounding merge to form a slave mentality. How do you untangle yourself from all that?

When I was admitted to treatment, my slave mentality held me captive and controlled me, burying my heart underground and forcing me to live from my head. Overcome by shame and self-hatred, I found myself trapped inside the very coping strategies the Enemy had assured would keep me safe. My heart needed to be exposed, both to me and to God, in order for reconditioning to happen.

During my last few weeks of treatment, two of my favorite therapists (we'll call them Z and D) asked if I would join them for a sand tray therapy session. I'd agreed somewhat blindly, unsure of what to expect. Deeply rooted in imaginative and subconscious expression, this unique form of therapy utilizes a tray of sand and toy figurines to help clients create scenes in a miniature world, often reflecting their own inner struggles and concerns. Sometimes clients know the scene they are creating. Other times, they don't. They simply place random figurines where they feel like they need to be, a scene unfolding before their eyes.

Honestly, I found the technique slightly odd. What could possibly be unveiled in me through a bunch of toy figurines in a sand tray?

Even after Z and D had explained this process to me, I'd chosen my figurines, and I'd placed them in the small tray of sand in front of me, my doubts remained. Hunched over this scene my subconscious had just created, my two therapists situated across from me, I told them I felt confused. In the dark. What did any of this symbolize?

In my sand tray, I'd placed huddles of tiny plastic people in three of the four corners. In one of the three corners, I'd placed a small stone house. A large eyeball, half-buried and reflecting specks of golden grittiness, occupied the center. In a circular pattern around the eyeball, I'd scattered a few aqua-blue stones.

In the fourth corner, I'd half-buried a lone figure: a girl in a blue dress, primed for defense, holding a sword. Trapped inside a bird cage.

Once I informed Z and D I had finished placing my figures, Z studied the sand tray quietly, gentle eyes pensive and fingers stroking his peppered-grey beard. Finally, he cleared his throat and began asking me questions. "Let's talk about the people. Just answer according to what feels right. Do you think they know each other?"

I studied them for a long moment. Something in me said *yes*. I nodded slowly.

"Do you think they know this girl with the sword?"

Again, *yes*.

Z paused again, gaze contemplatively traveling to each of the four corners of the sand tray. After a brief stretch of silence, he continued asking questions. "This girl under the bird cage is striking. My eyes keep going back to the image. Can she get out of the cage?"

I stared at her long and hard, mind working and fragmented thoughts spinning. "No, I don't think so."

As if Z could see the ramped inner workings of my brain, he relaxed into his chair and allowed the silence to linger. After a few moments, D entered the conversation, voice curious. "I noticed she's all alone. If she knows all the people in the other corners, why do you think she's not with them?"

I surveyed her sword. Her defensive posture. The bird cage enclosing her. Her calculated distance. My response came quickly, the words rolling off my tongue. "*She feels like she needs to protect herself.*" As my statement hung in the air, an internal light switch suddenly flipped on. Emotion began to build in me, twisting my stomach into knots. Understanding registered in my body. My mind lagged behind and attempted to catch up.

I scrutinized this lone figure, half-buried in sand, and felt Z peering deeply into me. Slowly, recognition seeped into his expression. He leaned forward, "Taylor, do you know who this girl represents?"

I didn't respond. Minutes slipped by as a tide of sadness rose and swelled in me, the pieces to my subconscious story fitting together. *That was me.* The sand blurred, tiny figurines swimming together and disappearing into Technicolor collisions. My tears pooled as the scene in front of me leaped to life.

Like a theater performance, the curtain had just been stripped away and I observed, as a spectator, my own world on display. Family, social circles, God, and my own sword-wielding, self-protecting, isolated, caged self.

For what felt like a long time, we sat in silence. Dumbfounded, I didn't know what to say. Pain lacerated, plunging through internal layers of self-protection I hadn't known existed until then. A knife plunged through my thick shell into hollowness. I felt empty inside. *When had I become her? What wounds did she carry? What patterns had she picked up to avoid pain? Was she anything more than this hardened shell she portrayed to her world?*

I didn't think so.

I'd heaped on layers of falseness for so long, I was sure whatever vestige of the real, vulnerable me that might remain had been buried in that sand long ago. God began to show me that these layers had to be peeled back, my hardened patterns cracked open, for a deep and restorative reconditioning. I had to open myself up to him, ask him to bring self-awareness, and allow him to reveal areas where I'd unintentionally fallen for the Enemy's schemes.

I now understand why God waited until those last few weeks of treatment to begin this reconditioning process in me. Quieted, defenses lowered, I'd finally stopped fighting him and demanding my own way. Why would any of us submit to a process this painful when we've oriented our whole lives around escaping pain? But broken and surrendered wills are God's birthing place for new things.

I left my sand tray session with Z and D, ruminating. How do I feel safe enough to step out of my cage? How do I even begin to lay down my sword? The darkness that had promised me safety now enslaved me. How do I break free?

> Maybe the key to standing up to darkness is stepping into the light, allowing God to root out the darkness in us in order to free us.

As we shed self-protection and offer up our swords of defense to God, choosing to step into vulnerability with him, he wields a different kind of sword: the sword of the Spirit. This sword (wielded *by the Spirit*) is the awakening voice of self-awareness. The Enemy's power over us weakens as we allow this sword to penetrate our hearts: cutting through tough and hardened layers and bringing exposure.[1]

This sword is the only offensive weapon listed in the armor of God (Eph. 6). While other pieces of armor provide external protection against the Enemy's schemes, the sword of the Spirit provides internal exposure to the sin and Enemy schemes *already binding us*. As the writer of Hebrews explained: "For we have the living Word of God [the Holy Spirit], which is full of energy, like a two-mouthed sword. It will even penetrate to the very core of our being where soul and spirit, bone and marrow meet! It interprets and reveals the true thoughts and secret motives of our hearts" (Heb. 4:12 TPT).

The Enemy tries to convince us to avoid the pain of exposure *at all costs* . . . especially exposure to God. He knows that his influence over us crumbles as we willingly lay our hearts before the Spirit of God for this painful, but deeply transformative, work. Well-known preacher Charles Spurgeon once explained that the sword of the Spirit cuts through bondage and slays our fears, doubts, despair, and disbelief, "hacking them to pieces," only after we allow this same sword to cut through us:

> The word of God in the hand of the Spirit wounds very
> terribly, and makes the heart of man to bleed. . . . That
> sword pursued you, and pierced you in the secrets of
> your soul, and made you bleed in a thousand places. . . .
> That wound was deadly, and none but he that killed
> could make you alive. . . . The Word gave you life; but
> it was at the first a great killer. Your soul was like a
> battle-field after a great fight . . . there is no weapon . . .
> so piercing, so able to divide between the joints and
> marrow, so penetrating as to the thoughts and intents of
> the heart.[2]

What kind of thoughts and intents of the heart does the sword of the Spirit primarily seek to reveal? To carve out the slave patterns in us, the sword of the Spirit illuminates specific Enemy lies that have taken root. Why? These lies birth the slave patterns (perfectionist, conformer, achiever, people pleaser) that wreak havoc on our lives.

In other words, every pattern directly correlates to a specific lie from the Enemy that we have believed and built our lives on.

Our slave patterns won't lose power by our forcibly willing ourselves out of the external action. We cannot free ourselves using self-effort. Our slave patterns lose power only as we allow the sword of the Spirit to dismantle the internal lie fueling the pattern. Diffusing lies. Infusing truth.

As Christian therapist Adam Young explains, the kingdom of darkness is opportunistic.[3] Remember how the Enemy offers us ways to cope with the cruelty of our world *in our weakest moments*? As our wounded hearts reel from our first experiences with pain, we grasp for meaning. We question why. Why did that happen? What does that mean? In these moments of vulnerability proceeding from callous remarks, absent parents, abuse, loss, or betrayal, he offers us meaning, an interpretation of the situation:

It's your fault.
Something's wrong with you.
You will never measure up.
You're a failure.
You're not enough.
You're such a hypocrite.
No one will ever love you.
You're stupid.
You deserve to be alone.
You're so dumb.
You've blown it again.
You will never truly belong.

As he floods us with personalized lies targeted toward specific wounds, he entices us to make unwitting agreements with him: *Yes, that's true. It's my fault. Yes. That's true. I will never belong. I will never be enough. I've blown it again. I am stupid. Something is wrong with me.* These lies blend into the cacophony of negative self-talk consuming us.

> Why are agreements so destructive? They are
> based not only on belief but on loyalty.

According to Young, "Agreements are not merely summary conclusions that you have agreed with based on the bad experiences in your life. You have unwittingly signed a legal document . . . breaking free from agreements that we have made is not simply a matter of correcting your wrong thinking. You can't just 'believe the truth' because you haven't just 'believed the lie.' You have agreed with it, binding yourself to evil."[4]

We initially make agreements with the Enemy to avoid future pain. Over the years, however, these agreements enslave us, shaping our perspectives and fueling self-protective patterns. Agreements orient our lives, drive our behavior, and determine our reactions and responses, especially in our closest relationships. They form the bedrock of the slave mentality.

The perfectionist strives for perfection at all costs because she has agreed with the Enemy that she is a failure.

The helper lives on "being needed" because she's agreed with the Enemy that no one will ever truly love her.

The conformer blends into her surroundings because she's agreed with the Enemy that she will never truly belong.

The achiever pursues success feverishly because she's agreed with the Enemy that she will never truly be enough.

Agreements also viciously prime our brains to anticipate future experiences based on past experiences of woundedness. Neuroscience and psychology show us that the way in which we experience the present is constantly being formed by memories from our pasts, many of which exist outside our awareness.[5] Many of us enter into conversations and situations unknowingly braced for what we think is going to happen. Our subconscious hyper-analyzes the actions, tones, and expressions of others as proving data. The moment our agreement is "proven," we avoid potential pain by immediately withdrawing. Overreacting. Giving up. These day-to-day occurrences only affirm our agreements and further bind us from living free.

As we allow the Spirit of God to awaken us to greater awareness, exposing the thoughts and intents of our hearts, we can begin to identify agreements. Paying attention to moments of tension, frustration, and discomfort is our first step forward. As we practice awareness of our thought cycles and physiological reactions in these moments, we'll begin to notice sentences and phrases that seem to come alive inside us. These phrases often indicate an agreement.

God wants to meet us here, infusing us with his Truth. The more we invite these agreements into our awareness, processing their deeper roots in our stories, the clearer our vision is to see our worlds on display. As we begin to recognize the childhood and soul wounds littering our pasts that have contributed to our struggle with anxiety, we have the opportunity to join God in writing a different story.

CHAPTER SEVEN

The Language of the Wounded Heart

*F*ather, I whispered softly in the dark, *Will you help me understand what's going on inside of me? All I know is that my wounds and struggles are destroying my life. Everything feels so confusing. Would you show me how to lay down my sword and step out of my cage? I need you to expose me to myself.*

I'd been hit with the startling reality of my sword-wielding, self-protecting, isolated, caged-in self a few hours before. Now, in a quiet room of sleeping faces, I wrestled with the decision in front of me. Would I smother this powerful sand tray experience with the next convenient distraction, numbing out and moving on? Or would I sit in my discomfort and confusion, waiting for and seeking understanding? Would I accept God's invitation into deeper awareness of my heart? As I lay awake in the early morning hours, my protective layers loosened. I felt him draw intimately near as I cautiously said *yes* to him. *Yes,* I think I want to go deeper. *Yes,* I think I want to see more. I think I'm willing to press into the pain of exposure.

As I accepted God's invitation into greater self-awareness, he gently began guiding me in an exploration of my own heart. Providing deeper insight into my story, he revealed themes, uncovering nuances of meaning, and exposed core agreements that fueled my anxiety and propelled me toward an eating disorder.

Together, we revisited a timeline of memories from almost every age of my life. As these moments resurfaced, they seemed to play before my eyes in slow motion, and I felt like I was observing myself from the outside. As God infused me with his perspective, I began to see peeking snippets of other slave patterns, driving my childhood behavior and sitting behind my teenage reactions and responses. Oh, Lord. Even these soft flickers of exposure hurt.

As I glimpsed at the slave mentality deeply embedded in my thinking, I hesitantly reconnected with parts of my heart that I'd dulled and forced dormant. God's tender presence remained heavy over me as I allowed unprocessed pain to surface.

On slow July afternoons, I'd often sit on the back-porch steps of my treatment facility under splashes of sunlight, journal open. As rays of sticky warmth spilled over me, truth seeped into my heart. Illuminating. Exposing. Unearthing. Rather than filling the external quiet with internal static, I asked God to help me sit in the silence. Sit with myself.

Briefly, I allowed myself to feel the pain of past disappointments, losses, rejections, and hurts. Both big and small. As I sank into the emotions of these painful memories, my anger often spiked, white-hot, against God. *Where were you? Why didn't you protect me? Why did you let that happen? How could that have possibly been your will?* In the brutal honesty of these moments, I also doubted myself. *How can you complain? Why can't you just get over it? You're just overreacting. How could you be so selfish and ungrateful?*

After two and half long months of intensive therapy, I was discharged from residential treatment. I was hopeful but still deeply hurting. And so tired of hurting. I wondered if this pain would ever lift. When I was admitted, I'd looked forward to discharge day, envisioning myself fully healed. I left smiling brightly (of course!) but inwardly aching. God was healing me, but in a different way than I expected. My family and I pulled out of the parking lot, and as I listened to the crunch of gravel under tires, I felt an unexpected pang of disappointment.

> One of the agreements I had made with the Enemy
> is that safety and authenticity cannot coexist.

I could be safe or I could be authentic (but never both, simultaneously). When I agreed with this lie, my life soon reaped destructive results. To protect myself from pain, I relinquished my authenticity, buried the real me, heaped on layers of falseness, wielded defensive coping strategies, and adapted into a hardened version of myself. As I continued to sit quietly in the rawness of my story, allowing God to expose slave patterns and agreements and infuse me with his truth, a small part of me began to long for authenticity.

My problem? I still didn't want anyone to see the real, struggling me.

I still ferociously avoided stepping into the truth of my whole story. I would rather minimize, stuff, block, deny, justify, rationalize, hide, and gloss over the parts I didn't like. Months after treatment, I hadn't looked one person in the eye and honestly talked to them about my battles with anxiety and anorexia. I also hadn't told anyone, even the people closest to me, about my sand tray experience or the deep processing that followed.

Rather, I hypervigilantly focused on appearing "completely fine." With fierce urgency, I overcompensated my "okayness" to myself and others. I threw frantic energy into assuring everyone how great I was. *Yes, I'm great. Everything's great. Life is great. No, I'm not struggling. Not at all!* These confident declarations could not have been further from the truth. But I was an expert smiler.

It seemed safer to put on a brave face than to admit how fragile I felt inside. It seemed safer to whisper *I'm fine* than to find words for wounds that I didn't yet fully understand myself and that filled me with inexplicable shame. When I operated in "picture-perfect mode," I could pick and choose which parts of my story I wanted to portray and which parts I wanted to gloss over (or completely edit out).

The more I longed for the unedited version of myself to be seen and known, the more intensely I grappled with shame and with my wild fear of rejection. To be fully myself with others, I had to openly acknowledge every part of my story. The painful parts. The unfixed parts. The traumatic parts. The shameful parts. The confusing parts. And the parts of me that still felt afraid and flawed and frustrated and failed and floundering and completely unfree.

I must not only sit in my woundedness but allow myself to be seen, wounded (which meant I had to acknowledge that I had been wounded and that I had wounds). I had to allow others to see the real me in the messy middle, when nothing made sense and everything seemed far from healed. This terrified me. Vulnerability was awkward, scary, uncomfortable, and outside the bounds of my perceived sense of control.

> Over the years, I had become adept at avoiding awkward. The rehearsed, masked, and polished version of me was lonely but felt much safer.

A few months after I was discharged from treatment, my family and I went on vacation in Florida. We were perusing a tourist shop one afternoon when I saw a sign for henna tattoos. For a few dollars, I could choose any design I wanted. Next to the sign, a college student, wearing a Hawaiian shirt, waist-length dreadlocks, and wrists full of neon friendship bracelets, listlessly scrolled on his phone. Leaning against a counter with a variety of colored henna pens, his sunken shoulders screamed *boredom* as he twirled a long piece of hair with his finger. Never in my life had I considered a tattoo, but as I studied the sign, an idea began to form.

The bustling shop milled with tourists as I reached for dollar bills in the back pocket of my jean shorts. Eyes laser-focused on the hippie with his henna pens, my legs moved without my permission, down the aisle and across the length of the store. When the hippie saw me walking toward him, he straightened and grinned, "Interested in a henna tattoo today?"

I nodded as he listed the price and colors. "How long will the tattoo last?" I asked, heart thumping.

"Usually about three or four days."

For a long moment, I paused and pretended to study the pens. Momentarily retreating inside myself, I warred with what seemed like a thousand conflicting emotions. My head told me that I had just gone crazy. However, among this cacophony of internal noise commanding me to turn around and leave, a gentle voice whispered encouragement. I pointed to the thin black pen and handed over cash, "Okay, I think I'll do it."

"What kind of henna do you want?"

I showed him a design on my phone.

"I've never seen that before. . . ." He studied the design closely. "What is it?"

The words stuck to my tongue as my mouth opened, then closed. I answered softly, "It's the eating disorder recovery symbol."

A spark of understanding flickered across his face, followed by an uneasy pause. Eye contact flittering, he nodded slowly, "Uh . . . okay. Sure. I can do that."

I held out my wrist, palm facing upward, as he drew black ink across pale skin: two curved swooshes, facing each other.

As I strolled the sandy seashore with my family later that evening, feeling exposed, I realized that I would never have gone through with the henna in a more familiar environment. The pain of potential rejection seemed too great in a circle of intimate faces. However, my henna felt less daunting in a sea of strangers. Although I still smiled widely, the inside of my wrist spelled out internal wounds. The inside of my wrist conveyed the message that my lips didn't yet know how to articulate: *I'm hurting. This is my story.*

The henna lasted barely three days, but by the time the first swoosh disappeared, I was ready for the other faded swoosh to come off too. No, thank you. I was done. Now I would go back to hiding. Standing over the bathroom sink of our hotel room, I wetted a bar of soap and rubbed the white block between my palms. Bubbles foaming, I ferociously scrubbed the soap into my wrist. As ink ran down my fingers and disappeared down the drain, my shoulders slowly released pent-up tension. I hunched over the sink, filled my lungs with air, and heaved a sigh of relief. Too painful. Too risky. I had tried to step into my full story, but I couldn't do it anymore. So I scrubbed it off. Retreating back inside myself, I walked out of the bathroom with a brave face and didn't take it off for the majority of the next three years.

> The dictionary defines "putting on a brave face" as "to behave as if a problem is not important or does not worry you."[1]

First, my brave face convinced me I wasn't actually that wounded. I was overreacting. My brain rationalized why I should be okay: I had a great childhood and no reason to complain. With calculated certainty, my brave face began to rationalize, justify, oversimplify, minimize, generalize, stuff, ignore, block, gloss over, and edit out all the pain in my story.

When my thoughts lingered too long on my sand tray experience, my brave face told me that self-reflection had been necessary during treatment. However, self-reflection was not a feasible or regular activity for busy, responsible, and productive people. I needed to reenter the real world. I needed to stop thinking about myself. How can I possibly think about that when children are dying of starvation somewhere in the world? There were bigger issues at stake.

According to my brave face, acknowledging wounds looked weak and caused me to appear naïve and overly sensitive. I mean, seriously. I just needed to pull myself together. Other people had lived through much more than I had. My brave face often shamed me for acting ungrateful and for my "glass-half-empty" mentality. No one enjoyed spending time with pessimistic people. I needed to be happy and thankful for what I did have.

After my brave face had thoroughly convinced me I was completely fine, it became relatively easy to convince other people too. I smiled and became a master at small talk, good eye contact, and pleasantries. My answer to the question "How are you?" was always the same: "I'm fine." Always, completely, totally, 100 percent *fine*.

According to my brave face, neediness was always an indication of weakness. Sometimes, my brave face instructed me to hide my limitations, calling this "self-reliance." Other times, my brave face instructed me to pretend like I had no needs, calling this "independence." Oftentimes, my brave face told me that no one should have to meet my needs, calling this "strength." And on days when I felt especially confident, my brave face congratulated me for outgrowing my needs, calling this "spiritual maturity."[2]

If someone saw through my brave face and asked how I was really doing, I quickly learned to respond with "I'm just tired" and emphasize my hectic schedule. And if I sensed a looming situation that might require vulnerability or indicate personal inadequacy, I learned to either excuse myself with an "I'm not feeling well," or emotionally detach myself from the situation and pretend I didn't care.

I learned that Sunday morning was the primary time for my exaggerated, spiritualized brave face. At church, I learned to smile wider and sing louder. (Because, according to my brave face, good Christians always smile and never struggle.) If my brave face felt especially difficult to muster, I'd hide behind a bathroom stall and wait until the redness disappeared from my eyes before I'd readjust my smile, unlock the door, and happily reenter the crowded auditorium of other widely smiling, loudly singing people.

During conversations with friends, I learned to engage in topics that were generally boring but relatively safe, surface-level, and appropriately shallow. If I ever found myself in a deepening spiritual conversation, I discovered the art of appearing vulnerable while not actually being vulnerable. My brave face assured me that God received the most glory from polished testimonies that hinted of struggles and wounds but always concluded with a glossy but-now-life-is-great ending.

According to my brave face, when anyone asked me if I had prayer requests, the appropriate response involved other people and generalized topics. I was allowed to request prayer for friends. Uncles. Aunts. Cousins. Grandparents. Pets. Sickness. Sleep. The weather. The economy. The health of our society. The state of our nation. Even the world. But my prayer requests could never be personal. I discovered that intimate relationships often led to accidental moments of vulnerability, so I avoided these relationships and maintained emotional distance. I avoided crying with others (and, when possible, avoided crying at all).

My brave face assured me that stuffing my pain, minimalizing my wounds, shaming myself for negative emotions, and always appearing completely fine is what brave actually looked like. I grew accustomed to pretending my wounded heart wasn't important and no longer impacted me. In my relentless attempts to prove my pain-free, picture-perfect life (to both myself and others), I didn't realize that my wounded heart was actually speaking all along: *"I'm fine. I don't need anyone."*

CHAPTER EIGHT

Running from Myself

For three years after treatment, I ignored my pain, stuffed my emotions, and prayed dutiful, happy prayers. My anxiety remained sky-high as I spent an exorbitant amount of time trying to convince my head of all sorts of things my heart hesitated to believe (like life was great and I actually wasn't struggling).

My brave-faced strategy worked well for a while. Unfortunately, I discovered that stuffed emotions and ignored pain don't magically vanish. Stuffed emotions progressively become jammed, squeezed, crushed, compressed, and lodged deep inside, fueling anxiety. The pain that once throbbed like an open, bleeding wound begins to toughen, scab, and harden. Or leak out, oozing like toxic poison on those around us.

The heavier and weightier my unprocessed pain grew, the more tirelessly my brain worked to rationalize why I should be okay. And in slivered moments of unguardedness, alone at night or awake in the early morning hours, I felt my brave face begin to slip and fracture around the edges. Sometimes, a wayward emotion became dislodged from the rock-solid mound in my chest and floated upward, forming an aching lump in the back of my throat. No, no, no. Panic swelled. I didn't want to go there. I didn't want to deal with that.

When a frenzied barrage of rationalizations wasn't enough to avoid pain anymore, I realized that some additional measures of precaution were necessary. If I crammed my days with nonstop activity and said yes to everything and everyone, my life became so chaotic with people and tasks and late nights and early mornings and lists and commitments and constant rushing that I no longer had time to think.

> I learned I could drown out the whispering cries of my wounded heart with a schedule stuffed with distractions.

In addition to assuring everyone I was completely fine, I once again detached myself from feeling any emotion and I threw my energy into constructing a shiny, plastic, I'm-fine-and-I-don't-need-you image. Gradually, the earsplitting voices of should and what-if and must-do began to dominate my mind and demand unrelenting hustle. A loud external world became the solution to numbing the ache of my internal world.

"Yes, I can do that!" and "Sure! Why not?" became my optimistic, I-have-it-all-together mantra that shaped my days and determined how I spent my time. I no longer controlled my schedule. Other people did. My never-say-no mentality barely allowed time between one commitment and the next. Although my hectic pace left me harried and frenzied and rarely present, I felt safer this way. Less wounded. More competent and capable. Whenever I glanced at my calendar and noticed a margin, any white space, my anxiety spiked. I remedied the problem as quickly as I could.

The voice of the Enemy (in the form of my inner critic) roared, a black vein of bitter self-hatred running through my body. What did I do? I grasped for more distractions and turned up the volume on my already chaotic life. I avoided any setting that involved silence, any slim opportunity where I might find myself stranded with unwanted thoughts. I played music in the shower, listened to podcasts on runs, called friends on drives, and typed papers in coffee shops that radiated noise: the whirl of espresso machines, the high-pitched murmur of dozens of voices, and the bustling activity of squeaking chairs and opening doors and zipping backpacks and clicking of keyboards. The deafening silence of the library made my skin crawl.

In long lines or during those excruciating minutes waiting for the next thing on my schedule, I scrolled through Instagram, responded to texts, and made to-do lists. My brain constantly spun with noise and static: not real, full thoughts, but whirling fragmented half-sentences and running lists of everything I would, should, and could do.

I stayed up late and woke early, utilizing caffeine to clear my foggy brain and cut through headaches. I grew accustomed to feeling jittery and weary and fragmented and drained. I pushed through when I was sick and ate on the run. I never truly rested on the weekends. My "resting" often included work, the gym, and my to-do list. I laser focused on the next thing. The next activity. The next noise I could reach for as a distraction. I was quickly turning once again into a frenzied ball of anxiety. Even when seated, I could never quite catch my breath. Silence, stillness, and slowness became my enemies. Noise, distraction, and chaos became the trifold axis around which my world relentlessly spun.

The honest, underlying truth? I was exhausted, yes, but I didn't really want to stop. My hectic schedule numbed me, distracted me, and was also my greatest source of affirmation. I prided myself in my packed, overbooked, bursting-at-the-seams, nonstop life because I was regularly praised for it. My professors applauded me for my grades, my friends admired me for my reliability, and church leadership commended me for my Christian service.

Deep down, do-gooding and people-pleasing and meeting needs made me feel valuable instead of vulnerable. Productivity, busyness, and responsibility (ideals I had always upheld, but now perched on the pedestal of idolatry) became the dimensions by which I measured my worth. I was the good girl. The dependable volunteer. The diligent student and hard worker, clamoring for her gold star from others, and from God.

But I never felt like his beloved daughter.

One morning, I walked into my therapist's office, sat down on her couch, and burst into tears. My therapist (we'll call her E) handed me tissues. She waited patiently for a few moments and then leaned forward. Her tone was soft, but firm: "Taylor, you're not allowing space in your schedule to breathe. Your pace is fueling your anxiety."

Without missing a beat, I responded between sobs, "No, you don't understand. I'm running away from my anxiety. If I slow down, my anxiety will catch up with me!"

Eyes widening slightly, E didn't respond. Rather, she allowed my words to sink into the following silence. Slowly, I realized how illogical that sounded. But it was true. The last few years after treatment had felt like a harried, frenzied, anxiety-driven chase. My slave mentality that had begun to emerge as I opened myself up to the Spirit of God was too painful. Too exposing. I didn't want to go any further. I began to realize that this inward journey is by no means a steady or linear process.

Stepping away from self-awareness, I'd attempted to move on by myself, on my own terms. I kept a fast-paced life, and whenever my schedule momentarily slowed, I'd begin to unravel, sucked down into a black hole of exhaustion-induced depression. I'd frantically smile and bat away pesky tears (because, of course, I was completely fine). As quickly as I could, I would recompose my brave face and promise myself I'd do better next time. I just needed to be more organized. More productive. Then, I'd inevitably repeat the cycle all over again.

Push too hard.

Begin to unravel.

Pull myself together.

Add a new self-help strategy.

Repeat the process.

Rather than rich or vibrant or deep, my life, in every dimension, felt thin and fake and surface level. I had no idea what I was feeling most of the time, but I couldn't deny that something felt deeply broken inside me. However, I wasn't quite ready to admit this yet (to myself or to my therapist). After forty-five minutes of justifying and explaining to E why I was actually "completely fine," she asked me to pull out my phone, open my calendar, and allocate one hour of space in the following week that I would intentionally leave open. No people. No plans. Nothing. I reluctantly agreed.

When the time came, I sat in my room, body rigid. As I watched the clock tick, my mind exploded with internal chatter (an ever-wandering, but always-running commentary on, well, basically, everything). Although I sat in silence, nothing about the experience felt quiet. Five minutes later, I pulled out my laptop and finished writing a paper. I feared sitting in silence, with my own thoughts. Most days, I felt like a mini tornado, whirling from one thing to the next.

> I constantly hustled and hoped that if I just ran fast enough, I could escape the unprocessed pain heavy in my chest.

Few of us know what to do with stillness, silence, and slowness. Sometimes, it seems like the better part of our society spins on the axis of noise, distraction, and chaos. Author and therapist K. J. Ramsey explains that busyness is the way most people instinctively seek to silence their shame.[1] In an effort to silence our feeling of inadequacy and sense of insufficiency, we revert to an overstuffed schedule that screeches with noise.

Often, following those moments of disorienting self-awareness, when we begin to touch the mystery of what is most real in our lives and stories, is when we tend to revert back into "normalcy" (or excessive busyness!) again. As if the exposure touched a raw nerve inside us, we can feel threatened and rebound into self-sufficiency, fiercely attempting to regain our sense of control.[2]

We go to the gym, binge-watch TV, volunteer, work late, spend time with friends, sleep, shop, clean, eat, diet, text, scroll through Instagram, and squeeze one more thing into our day. Many of us attempt to outrun our fear of silence by frantically rushing from one thing to the next. Others avoid silence without moving at all. Escaping through social media, TV, and Netflix, they numb the pain of their realities by temporarily entering into another person's world or a make-believe story, often with a fairy-tale ending.

Even when our schedules are cleared and Netflix is turned off, our internal worlds often still clatter with noise: to-do lists, snippets of previous conversations (and all the things we wish we had or hadn't said), hypothetical scenarios, what-ifs, worries, negative self-talk, insecurities, and all the things we could have been, should have been, or wished we were doing. External silence can rarely be equated to quiet.

The trickiest, most stronghold-like thing about it all is that working and cleaning and volunteering and going to the gym are not bad ways to spend our time. Activities like these are good. Even necessary. But this is where the Enemy works. The Enemy can twist good things in our lives into the very hindrances that prevent us from entering into the abundant life God offers us. Rather than the blatant sins, his most destructive work occurs in the subtle mind-set shifts, the half-truths, the white lies, and the external image. He works in misplaced identities and skewed purposes and dual motives.

God cares most about our inner lives. The Enemy cares most about our image. And when we begin to buy into the Enemy's lie that our external life is more important than who we are on the inside, we often begin to use good, God-ordained things in destructive ways (like running as far away from our insides as possible).

When volunteering or sleeping or going to the gym or do-gooding become more about escapism and promoting a false persona, they become like drugs: ways to anesthetize ourselves from feeling pain and facing our reality.[3] Our real selves. They become the very means by which we construct our own I'm-fine-and-I-don't-need-you images. They numb us and become addictive. In an already fast-paced and flashy world, where "I'm so busy" is met with affirmation, "I'm exhausted" is often viewed as an accolade of success, and binge-watching a show on Netflix is considered socially acceptable, why would we ever want to stop?

We can hide our real selves and construct convincing personas with alarming ease, which is part of the reason why authenticity is so difficult! Promoting a polished, false image is much easier and feels safer than vulnerability. But in my attempts to avoid pain and promote a less wounded version of myself, I found myself exhausted and disconnected from all the things that truly mattered: My own heart. My whole story. The people closest to me. God. I'm learning that when we all frantically focus on maintaining a picture-perfect exterior, no one is given permission (or feels like they have permission) to reach out and be real with others or with God.

Few of us know how to sit with ourselves in both external and internal silence. Most of us don't want to. The idea of releasing the tension from our necks and shoulders and sitting with our own thoughts sounds terrifying. When we are alone and in silence, the noise fades, our brave face crumbles, and uncomfortable emotions rise. All the things we're trying not to think about begin to surface without our control.

> In silence, sitting with ourselves, we
> hear our wounded hearts cry.

I will not fall apart. I will hold it together. I will be fine. These thoughts circled in my mind as I headed for a visit home. I sensed that I had pushed too hard and dug too deep into my energy reserves again. I desperately wanted to avoid another cycle where I would begin to unravel and then have to pull myself together again. I didn't realize how exhausted I truly was until I arrived home. I didn't "begin to unravel." I just unraveled. I was done. As my pace momentarily slowed, I felt weighed down and lethargic. My body informed me that it couldn't stuff any more unprocessed emotions. How is it possible to feel so emotionally stuffed and empty at the same time?

At first, I fought the unraveling, attempting to pull myself back together. Slowly, I began to realize that I couldn't do it anymore. Then, I began to realize how tired I was of trying to keep it all together. My brave face began to crack, then fracture, and then crumble, eventually sliding off completely. I didn't have the energy to manufacture any more noise. As unwanted emotions and unwelcomed thoughts overwhelmed me, I began collapsing in on myself.

One morning, I woke up early and slipped downstairs to our back patio to watch the sunrise. Settling into a cushioned chair, fingers laced around a mug of coffee, I watched the horizon turn into a vibrant canvas of color. As splashes of pinks and purples intermingled with gold, I closed my eyes and felt the sun's warmth against my face. My mind traveled to all those afternoons on the back-porch steps of my treatment facility. Sitting in the summer sun, I had felt connected with God and with myself as I had allowed memories to surface, journaling and praying. I had felt like I was beginning to wake up to myself. Life was slowly becoming more playful, and less rigid. More gray, less black and white. More grace, less judgment.

A sickening ache formed in the pit of my stomach as I realized how detached and hardened I felt: hardened laughter, hardened smiles, hardened side comments, hardened thoughts, hardened perspective, and hardened prayers. What had happened over the last few years, since my heart had been so open and tender and receptive to God?

Now, everything about me felt brittle and fake, fueling criticism and cynicism. My desperation to be okay had turned into a stubborn form of self-reliance and self-dependence. My "I-don't-need-you" mentality had gradually shifted into an "I-must-be-all-that-I-need" mentality. In my striving to keep it all together, pride lingered. I sat on our back patio for a long time. In this rare moment of both external and internal silence, my gaze slowly turned inward. I began to peer into the darkness, and when I did, questions surfaced.

Does someone see me?

Am I worthy of love?

Do I have value?

Am I safe?

Does my existence even matter?

As a plunging sense of inadequacy washed over me, I felt defeated and discouraged. Shame clawed at my soul, and I whispered softly, *I'm sorry, Jesus. I'm so sorry.* But, oddly, the only sense of disappointment I felt was from myself.

CHAPTER NINE

Scrubbed Clean and Crawling

I wrestled with a sweeping wave of aloneness. My questions of worth and value resounded sharply and faded quickly, with a staccato echo across what seemed like an empty, cavernous void. Self-sufficiency had seemed seductively alluring at first. I had discovered that constructing an I'm-fine-and-I-don't-need-you image seemed safer than settling into the slow, painful, frustrating inward journey with God. I still wanted to live a godly life and receive his blessings, but I wanted to do it my own way, how I wanted, on my own terms.

Since scrubbing off my henna and pulling on my brave face, I had attempted to be a good person who did Christian things, used Christian words, and tried not to sin. I could make myself worthy. I could do the Christian life on my own, without the messy, painful inner work. Managing the externals felt less risky and looked more shiny and spiritual. I hadn't realized I was really just flaunting the same message to God: *I'm completely fine and I don't need you.* My rebellious declaration of independence is the definition of sin.

Initially, my pain-numbing, tornado-spiraling way of navigating life had felt luxuriously freeing, like a deep exhale from all the heaviness. I enjoyed the addictive sense of power and control that independence had offered me. I hid behind my brave face, freely stuffed my schedule with distractions, and selected which parts of my story I wanted to portray to promote a glossy, picture-perfect version of myself. The self that God and others would love. However, as I sat on our back patio, shoulders hunched in weary defeat, I realized I didn't feel in control anymore. Rather, I felt dangerously out of control. Other people dictated my schedule, and anxiety dominated me.

With perfectionistic, panic-fueled hustling, I had tried to please God, please others, be a good person, and keep my life well-managed, orderly, and controlled, all on my own, by my own effort. Rather than a Father, I viewed God more as a critical taskmaster, peering down at me from heaven and keeping score of all the good and bad things I did. With well-intended (but misguided) diligence, I strived to become the person I thought I should be, live how I thought I should live, and do all the things I thought I should do.

I was rarely real with others, and I certainty wasn't real with God.

I performed for him in order to prove my worthiness and earn his approval: *I am worthy of love! I am worthy of acceptance! Do you see me, God? I'm doing good things for you! I am being a good person for you!* However, I didn't like the hardened, anxiety-riddled person I had to become to sustain that externally polished (but internally crumbling) life of nonstop rushing and worrying and noise and chaos. I didn't want to be that person anymore. I was weary of trying to hold my world together.

> In all my strenuous self-efforts to please God,
> I had never felt more disconnected.

A few months later, I traveled to Costa Rica on a mission trip with a small team from my church. Our team was housed by a local missionary family who graciously organized ministry events and provided transportation. Our schedule stayed busy, and we often woke before six o'clock, teaching English and facilitating children's programs in national schools and churches well into the evening.

One afternoon, a ministry event was suddenly canceled, and we found ourselves with an hour of unexpected free time. Already in the bustling city of Cartago, we bused a short distance down dusty streets to a famous cathedral, known as the Basilica of Our Lady of the Angels. Sticky with heat and skirt hem already covered in a thin layer of mud, I gladly fell in step with the crowd already filing in through massive, creaking doors. The cathedral was cool and dimly lit, soaked with the pungent smell of burning incense.

I wasn't prepared for what I was about to see.

As my eyes slowly adjusted from the blistering sun, I observed my surroundings. The architecture was magnificent. A high dome ceiling displayed ornate mosaics of gold and vibrant reds, and the same rich colors and intricate patterns coated thick pillars in each corner of the expansive sanctuary. Small windows projecting slivers of natural sunlight framed the dome, but the cathedral's soft glow came mostly from hundreds of candles, lining almost every flat surface and casting the entire space in flickering light. Wooden pews neatly lined the cathedral's center. Behind a white railing toward the front of the room stood a simple cross.

Chin tilted upward, I observed my surroundings slowly, mesmerized by the exquisite artwork covering almost every square inch of the massive building. Eyes running the length of the ceiling, my gaze traveled downward, past the dome, past the hand-painted arches and beams, to the central aisle. My breath caught in my throat. In solemn lines, dozens of people crawled, slowly inching toward the cross.

Without shifting my gaze, I tapped one of the local missionary's shoulders and whispered, "What are they doing?"

His response came quickly, tone holding notes of sadness, "They're crawling to prove to God their piety. When they reach the cross, they pray and hope that their good performance has warranted God's favor."

Emotion stirred in me as I slipped into a back pew. Leaning forward, I rested my elbows on my knees and cupped my face with my hands. I had never seen anything like it before. Time stilled as I sat, speechless, and watched a sea of fear-laced faces and questioning eyes gradually shuffle to the cross.

The men wore long pants and ironed shirts: bodies washed, jaws shaved, dark hair neatly parted and slicked back. The women wore knitted shawls around their shoulders and long, colorful skirts. With scrubbed faces, children lingered and waited, peering out with anxious eyes. A small girl stood near the entrance, eyes laser-focused on her crawling mother as she sucked her thumb and squeezed a cloth doll tightly against her chest. She wore what looked like a combination of her best, polished shoes.

The atmosphere was somber and dark, thick with desperation. I could almost feel the pain, see the worried thoughts running through minds, as dozens stilled in prayer, stooped on hands and knees, and began the long crawl down the length of the cathedral toward the cross.

My attention was captured by an older couple entering the sanctuary. The woman hobbling slightly ahead, her gnarled, purple-veined hands clutching a cane. Gait unsteady, she paused for a moment, regaining her balance, before handing her cane to her husband. Her shawl slipped off one shoulder as she lowered herself to the floor, body trembling. She winced as her knees pressed against the marbled floor. Her husband bent and whispered into her ear, stooping to support her. She shook her head firmly, pushing him away, chin set and back arched in determination.

But I saw her eyes.

They glistened with fear and uncertainty. In the lines of unspoken pain creasing this old woman's face, I glimpsed an anguished soul: *Have I been good enough to deserve God's favor? Will God actually hear me among these masses? How is it that I can kneel before the cross of Christ and he still feels so far away?*

I didn't realize I was crying until droplets fell from my chin, landing in tiny splashes on the mosaic tiled floor. My silent tears quickened, running messily down my face as if something had burst in the deepest part of me. The Father's whisper cut through the stillness. His voice was gentle, intimate, and drenched in affection . . . *Taylor, my daughter. Look. Do you see her? That is how you approach me, too.*

As I watched this woman crawl, I saw myself in her. I didn't know her story, but I resonated with her demeanor toward God. It was as if we both gazed at the cross, hearts crying out, *Am I good enough? Am I worthy of your love and acceptance?* This woman appeared so neat and tidy and clean. So spiritual. She had washed away the filth and grime and put on her best clothes. With a polished exterior, she approached God on hands and knees, wondering if she had been good enough to earn his favor. *Oh, Lord. Yes. That was me, too.*

> I also believed God only loved the pretty and clean and perfectly packaged and super-spiritual version of me.

I believed he was pleased with me on good days, when I was kind and loving and noble, and did all the things I was supposed to do. On bad days? In the midst of failures and habitual sin and shameful thoughts and twisted motives and raw insecurity, I envisioned his (at best) displeasure and (at worst) rejection.

As I watched this woman, I realized that I internally approached God just like she was: crawling. In almost every area of my life, I worked for approval, trying to prove my worth and earn love with self-effort. My brokenness and weakness disgusted me, and I believed that brokenness and weakness disgusted him, too. I believed he viewed the parts of myself that I deeply disliked with similar criticism. The parts of my story that filled me with immobilizing fear and shame, I believed were shameful for him, too.

My mind wandered back to eighteen-year-old me, standing over a hotel bathroom sink as I washed off the eating disorder recovery symbol. I remembered the stubborn expression on my face as I fiercely scrubbed my wrist until the skin reddened. That henna had spoken of internal wounds, parts of me that I deeply disliked, and parts of my stories that filled me with shame.

When I'd rubbed off the skin-deep ink, I realized something had happened inside me on the heart level. I had rejected a part of myself: my wounded self. I loathed my scars and faults, and the unfixed, painful, and messy areas of my life. Authenticity terrified me, and I'd anxiously recoiled from my own God-ordained story. Why? Like this woman, I only felt safe with God when I saw myself as lovable, good, and worthy of his affection, without scars or fears or tears or struggles. Basically, perfect.[1]

> I spoke about the unconditional love of God with my lips, but my heart still believed that God's love had conditions for me.

In Luke 15, Jesus tells a story about a son and his father. The story begins with the son demanding an early inheritance and traveling to a distant land, quickly squandering all the money. After his own version of I'm-fine-and-don't-need-you living, he finds himself penniless and homeless. As he sits in a pigpen, eating animal slops, he realizes that he doesn't want to live this way anymore. His way had failed him miserably.

Sitting in that Costa Rican cathedral, I realized I didn't want to live in self-dependence and self-reliance anymore either. I was exhausted from striving to maintain a polished exterior. I couldn't fake smile any longer. As I surveyed the condition of my heart, I realized that my way had failed me miserably, too. I was not completely fine.

Just like the father in the story of the prodigal son, God had known all along that my way would fail. He knows that our way always fails us, 100 percent of the time. But on the basis of his desire for genuine relationship, he allows us choice. He knows we will never willingly choose his way unless we have utterly failed in our own attempts. Why? An "I'm-fine-and-I-don't-need-you" mentality is deeply ingrained in all of us. It's the defining condition of our fallen, human nature. We *all* are naturally bent toward our own way, *all the time.*

He aches at the disconnection, yet he allows us to live life without him (although we never truly leave his hands). He grieves as many of us attempt to live the Christian life on our own: performing, striving, and crawling to prove our worth and earn his love and acceptance. He weeps over our self-rejection, shame, and self-loathing. Patiently, he waits for us to come to the end of ourselves: unraveled and weary. Only then, when we finally stop running from ourselves, will we go to him, broken, and realize that his love is not based on us. We cannot make ourselves worthy. His love was never determined by our worthiness. *Look at the cross!*

He whispers. *Don't you see that I've loved and accepted you always, exactly as you are?*

As the prodigal son sat in the pigpen, he thought of the security and comfort of his father's house. After seeing where his self-dependence had brought him, he recognized his unworthiness to even be called a son. With threadbare clothes, covered in muck and smelling like pigs, he returned home just as he was. The Father's response?

> From a long distance away, his father saw him coming,
> *dressed as a beggar,* and great compassion swelled up
> in his heart for his son who was returning home. The
> father raced out to meet him, swept him up in his arms,
> hugged him dearly, and kissed him over and over with
> tender love. (Luke 15:20 TPT—emphasis in original)

Overwhelmed by his father's affection toward the real, dirty, broken him, he confessed, "'Father, I was wrong. I have sinned against you. I could never deserve to be called your son. Just let me be—' The father interrupted and said, 'Son, you're home now!'" (Luke 15:21 TPT). Sweeping his own coat over his son's threadbare shoulders, he slipped a ring on his finger that sealed his sonship, and they celebrated. No condemnation. No judgment. No rejection. Not even a fleeting look of disapproval or disappointment over wasted years, poor decisions, and past mistakes. Only tears of joy, eyes brimming with pure delight, and kisses of mercy.

As I sat on that pew in Costa Rica, I began to uncurl and unmask before God. I realized that I wanted to go home. I didn't want to crawl anymore. In all my striving and performance and "fine-ness," I had attempted to hide my woundedness. But God had seen all of me, all along, and loved all of me from the beginning. As my tears streamed, I felt my unworthiness deeply and realized that he still accepted me freely, compassionately, and fully.

Nothing I could do would make me worthy of his love, for his love was never based on me.

Father, I want to come home, my heart cried in the darkened corner of that cathedral. Internally, the real me, the broken and dirty and flawed me, went before him without hiding. When I finally stopped running from myself, I felt him run to me. When I finally came into the present, bringing all of me into the open, I came into the present with God. As I sat with myself, I realized that I was sitting with him, too. The warmth of his presence overwhelmed me.

As if he had pulled me into the tightest embrace, I felt him place both hands on my face and lean close, staring deep into my eyes with such pure and unashamed affection that it made my heart want to burst. *I'm so sorry, Lord. I'm not completely fine and I desperately need you. I know I'm not worthy. . . .* But the Father interrupted me. *You are my daughter, and I love you. You are home now!*

Right in the middle of my wounded heart, I felt love begin to swell. I began to realize that the acceptance I had been looking for all along came from not an external source, but an internal space. The love I longed for was not discovered in the searching but in the stillness, as I simply created space for it. Rather than frantic striving, spotless performance, or flawless spirituality, I had encountered the love of God most profoundly in a quiet moment, in the secret place of me freely going to him just as I was. All of me and my past story.

CHAPTER TEN

Waking Up to the Color

The rumpled pages of my Bible lay open to Genesis. I'd returned home from Costa Rica late the night before. Up early, I'd slipped outside while the house was still quiet. My world was encased in hues of warm grey, singing with the promise of another sunrise. I breathed in deeply and exhaled slowly, settling back and opening my thick leather-bound journaling Bible.

This cracked concrete-floored patio, with its shaded awning and faded yellow-cushioned seating, was becoming my haven. My secret place. I felt peaceful here, staring out into a trimmed lawn with green foliage and listening to the melodious calls of morning birds.

For the first time in a long time, the silence was beginning to feel safe.

I had carefully thumbed to the first few pages of Scripture, and I read the words slowly, letting their meaning sink deep. I read how the Spirit of the Lord had hovered, commanding light into existence. I read how he spun the universe into motion, his hands weaving together galaxies, igniting the sun and shaping the moon, aligning planets, painting the delicate wings of butterflies, crafting the leathery skins of reptiles, and unfolding the glimmering scales of sea creatures. I envisioned his Spirit dancing behind the majestic, pounding waterfalls and lingering in ocean depths. I thought about how, with a single thought, he had established the patterns of migration, the cadenced cycle of seasons, and the fragile bounds of human time. In Genesis 2, I read how he fashioned Adam from dust, placing his just-formed body in the garden of Eden and breathing life into his lungs.

My heart wondered at this God who tethered the winds and tamed the night sky into a canvas of sparkling beauty. He was the same God who had drawn close to me in that Costa Rican cathedral, whispering love and holding me. Now these words rang less about the account of creation and more about the reality of God: the breathtaking artistry of his fingers and the rhythmic pulsing of a divine heartbeat.

God is real. He's alive. He's here. He's close, intimate, and present.

Each sentence strung together, testifying to a living God who wanted to be known. Each page painted him in a swirling shroud of mystery. I glimpsed a Person who spoke and who longed to be discovered. Each chapter felt invitational, and my soul felt more alive when I saw God in the same way. There was a hopeful quickening to my spirit and a sweet sense of homecoming to the restless yearning and empty aching of my heart. I felt more grounded and settled, less anxious and rattled, when I viewed my small life through the lens of this all-powerful but deeply personal Creator.

> This Creator God desires to walk intimately with us, offering us a place of rest, connection, and safety.

For the first time in years, I felt deeply aware of his presence with me, but my heart questioned, *How do I stay here?* I reflected on my intimate encounter with God in the cathedral. *How do I stay in that place of love?* As I finished Genesis 2, I imagined Adam and Eve walking with God in the cool afternoon breeze of the Garden, laughing and talking. As I lingered in the devastation of Genesis 3, I pictured them hiding from him in fear and shame after the fall.

The last few years had felt like a white-knuckled chase to meet expectations, hustle to please, and rush from one thing to the next at backbreaking speed out of a wild, unmanaged place of anxiety. The disconnection I felt from my body and emotions seemed almost normal. At the expense of never saying no and living beyond my own limits, I had avoided feelings of shame and guilt at all costs. *How do I stay connected with you, Father? I want to, but I don't know how. I am so easily distracted by other things. I am so easily disconnected from you by my own fear and hiding.* Jesus's response is in the gospel of Matthew:

> Are you tired? Worn out? Burned out on religion? Come to me. Get away with me and you'll recover your life. I'll show you how to take a real rest. Walk with me and work with me—watch how I do it. Learn the unforced rhythms of grace. I won't lay anything heavy or ill-fitting on you. Keep company with me and you'll learn to live freely and lightly. (Matt. 11:28–30 *The Message*)

Unforced rhythms of grace. My soul breathed deeply at the words, and I heard echoes of the Garden in his invitation. I sensed him lovingly welcoming me to a slower, deeper kind of life with him. *Yes, Jesus, yes. I'm weary of running from myself. Please teach me how to walk with you instead. Please show me how to live freely and lightly.*

During Jesus's earthly ministry, he often visited the home of two sisters named Mary and Martha. Along with their brother Lazarus, they are described as some of his closest friends. The Gospel of Luke records an interaction between the two sisters and Jesus during one of his visits to their home. When describing this story, the apostle takes noticeable effort in emphasizing Mary and Martha's responses to Jesus. Why?

They could not be more different.

The story begins with Jesus traveling to their village with his disciples. As the men pile into Mary and Martha's home after a long day of travel, I imagine them thirsty, sweaty, and hungry. Jesus sits down and immediately begins to teach, and Mary sits down next to him, attentively absorbing every revelation he shared. However, Scripture notes that Martha continues to spin circles around Jesus, quickly becoming exasperated with finishing numerous household chores and preparations for their guests.

Eventually, she interrupted him: "Lord, don't you think it's unfair that my sister left me to do all the work by myself? You should tell her to get up and help me" (Luke 10:40 TPT).

Jesus's gentle response to Martha shook me.

"Martha, my beloved Martha. Why are you upset and troubled, pulled away by all these many distractions? Mary has discovered the one thing most important by choosing to sit at my feet. She is undistracted, and I won't take this privilege from her" (Luke 10:41–42 TPT).

I sat in this short exchange between Martha and Jesus deeply, studying her words. Soaking in his response. As rainy June afternoons folded into blistering July heat, my heart anxiously skipped with the prospect of another busy season (where my sacred internal shifting would clash with the stark reality of my external life). Doesn't Martha's bustling preparations and busy planning seem like proper, appropriate, and normal responses? Look at the good things she was doing for Jesus! And don't her complaints about Mary seem, well, slightly legitimate?

Jesus's response to Martha: Choose me.

What? Really? Jesus would rather have her sit with him than serve him?

I began to wonder, how often do I run around for Jesus, doing all sorts of things that he never asked me to do? How often do I interrupt him and anxiously demand *I need help!* for something that he never requested of me? All while I wrestle with the festering underlying motives of fear, insecurity, bitterness, and questioning what other people think. I had compassion for Martha because I saw myself in her.

> My distraction-fueled life had prevented me from giving Jesus my attention.

In her book *Try Softer*, author and therapist Aundi Kolber explains that our ability to set good limits is inseparably linked to our felt sense of safety. If we don't feel safe, we will struggle to set appropriate boundaries in our lives.[1] Addressing three different kinds of safety, Aundi describes safety in our bodies as feeling solid, responsive, and aware; safety in our relationships as connection, vulnerability, and trust; and safety with God as connection, belonging, and mystery.[2]

As I studied the responses of Mary and Martha in this passage, I recognized that *Mary had clearly felt safe with Jesus and safe with herself.* She felt safe enough to set boundaries that had already prepared her with the time, emotional capacity, and groundedness to be present with him in this moment. She was comfortable with her no. I began to see that I had an inner-Martha response and inner-Mary response to his invitation to relationship. Slowly,

I saw the outworking of these two contrasting responses to Jesus littering my day.

The inner-Martha response orients herself around *doing*. Her approach to life: White-knuckled. Image-conscious. Anxiety-riddled. She keeps a grinding pace and often feels enslaved to inner compulsions and held captive to outer expectations. Her mouth always says *yes*, even when her gut screams *no*. She focuses on her appearances and constantly wonders what other people think. *Do they like me? Am I accepted? What do they actually think about me?* She is often consumed with preserving and protecting the most external, visible layers of herself. Leaving her emotions unacknowledged and unaddressed, she tends to her image at the expense of an unkempt and untended soul.

She fears risk and the unknown, planting herself firmly in the polished, expected, and predictable. She actively seeks to maintain control. Her schedule keeps her too busy, too frazzled and uptight, to hear Jesus's voice or to notice his presence. She longs to be a good person, but insecurity causes her to define her value by the impressiveness of her external life. Underneath all her striving lies a deep-rooted belief in the voice that calls her *worthless* and *unlovable*. Her emotions are often shaped by the attractive countersolutions of people-pleasing, productivity, popularity, perfectionism, and power. She bases her worthiness on what she does and is much more focused on results than relationship.

The inner-Mary response orients herself around *noticing what God is doing*. She leans into her relationship with him. Her approach to life: Rhythmic. Reflective. Lighthearted. Although her life stays full, she allows the Spirit to guide her schedule (rather than allowing her schedule to control her), and her gentle acceptance of her own limitations allows her to say yes and no to requests freely. *Has God called me to that right now? Does this align with my priorities? Do I have the space and capacity?* She doesn't wear masks or pretend to be someone she is not. She is genuine, open, and humble. She is keenly aware of her own emotions and consistently brings frustrations, disappointments, and resentments to God. *Why am I feeling this way, Lord? Can you help me understand?* She knows that her truest self emerges from a well-tended soul.

She remains attentive and attuned to God throughout her day, still and quiet in the context of her relationship with him. Rather than demanding, pleading, or shouting anxious requests, she listens instead for his voice of guidance and direction. She isn't afraid of silence and enjoys the smallest details of her day: the sunrise, the flowers on the roadside, the encouraging words from a friend. She knows these are all blessings from God, gentle reminders of his beautiful, strong, but quiet voice that calls her his beloved.[3]

Like Martha, how often are we too distracted to notice Jesus's instruction, his nearness, and his whispers of tender love? How often are we so consumed with the noise, chaos, and activity radiating from our lives that we miss his presence and daily blessings, filling our lives and spilling over into each day? How often does our inner-Martha response determine our thinking and behaviors, causing us to care more about our external worlds than our souls?

Jesus is always speaking, always calling us deeper, always inviting us to discover more of himself. He's always beckoning us away from self-protective tendencies or performance and into the present moment with him. What defined Mary's connection with Jesus? When he spoke, she listened. When he drew near, she leaned in. And she felt safe enough in his arms, safe enough inside her own skin, to set limits that allowed her to do so. Mary and Martha's story shows us that our love for God is measured not by our frantic activity but by our focused attention.

Jesus calls each of us into this rhythmic pattern of coming and going. Coming into his presence, going out into the world.[4]

Coming into his presence, carrying his peace and inner stillness into the rest of our day. We experience God most powerfully not in the locus of bustling action, chaos, and noise, but in these quiet moments of coming to him just as we are.

We must create space for coming.

I am not good at this. Like Martha, I am so easily swept away and distracted by other, less important things. I go, go, go until I'm depleted and dry, and I struggle to stop, slow down, and sit with Jesus. I'm not naturally drawn to silence or stillness or slowness. However, I'm learning that consistently retreating into still and quiet moments with God is what prevents me from trying to escape life. While escape leads to disconnection from God, myself, and others, retreat leads to intimacy, wholeness, and growth.

Healing from pain, woundedness, and wrong thinking happens in the margins of life—in the quiet, as we willingly sit with Jesus and others in the unfixed, painful, and messy. As we consistently bring our real selves into the open before God, we begin to discover the true God (and our true selves) again. While anxiety can cause me to feel instantly threatened and ungrounded, throwing me into what-if and worst-case-scenario thinking, I have to keep internally reminding myself to connect to the present: *I am safe. I have a choice. I can say no. God is with me. I am not alone.* I have to continually practice settling my soul and choosing to be quiet.

> As I connect with God in the moment, I find myself connected to peace.

During one of my first few days in residential treatment, I received a letter from a family friend. She had known me since I was a little girl and frequently watched my sister and me on Thursdays. We'd swim together on hot afternoons, and on rainy days, she'd pull out thick, white sheets of paper and a basket of crayons. We would sit around her kitchen table and draw. When I finished each picture, I'd sign my name in big, scrawling letters, and she'd slide the picture into a folder, labeled with my name.

When I received her letter in treatment years later, I peeled back the envelope flap carefully. She had written me a short note: She was praying for me. She loved me. And she'd included a picture I had drawn over a decade ago. The neatly folded picture fell into my lap, and I opened it slowly. Emotion rose in my throat as I stared down at an explosion of colors. Pinks, purples, greens, yellows, reds, oranges, and blues splashed across the page. The picture displayed a messy eruption of crooked lines and polka-dots. Fingering the paper sadly, I realized how detached I felt from this younger, freer version of myself.

She had been fully alive. She had been fully living.

In a moment of spontaneity, I grabbed crayons and flipped to a fresh page of my journal. I drew the same picture again, tears intermingling with chalky lines and polka-dots as I drew brightness across blankness, one color at a time. With each turquoise swirl and stroke of emerald green, God whispered into my heart's vulnerable places: *I will restore color to your life*, he told me. *One color at a time.*

Three years later, I remembered that picture and that God-given promise. I hadn't fully grasped its meaning then, but now I was finally beginning to understand. For so long, my life had seemed empty, dull, and hollow: void of light and deadened to the reality of God. I wanted more of him, to know him as his beloved.

Eventually, I began trying to sit with myself and God for five minutes each day. Just five minutes. I'd sit at my desk each morning and breathe deeply. Inhaling. Exhaling. Allowing my emotions to catch up with me and taking them to God, one by one. I would remind myself that he was with me in that moment, allowing this truth to penetrate. *Be still and know that he is God. . . . Be still and know that he is God. . . .* I'd repeat to myself and over and over and over again. I envisioned Mary sitting at Jesus's feet, and I asked him to help me notice his nearness, his blessings, his voice.

Most of the time, my mind wandered into the realm of to-do lists and should-dos before half the time was up. Some days, my racing brain never slowed and I'd jump up from my desk in a huff of anxious frustration. *How do I stay here with God?* I kept coming to him and carving out space for connection. I would just sit. Fill my lungs with air and exhale deeply. Be quiet. Take a slow walk outside. Feel the gentle breeze.

With awkwardness, I began to learn how to say no to other things. When tension snaked through me at a commitment that I knew God hadn't called me to, I stuttered an "I'm sorry, but I can't right now. . . ." Instead of guilt, relief flooded me every time. Haltingly, my overstuffed schedule slowed to a more sustainable rhythm.

Over time, the spinning anxiety threatening to consume me also began to slow. Although I still kept a full schedule, each day held more margin: enough time to walk leisurely, feel the sun on my skin, taste the food I was eating, say yes to a spontaneous afternoon with friends, go to bed early, sip a good cup of coffee slowly, notice a fleeting emotion in the eyes of the person sitting across from me. When I finally stepped into the present with God and with myself, my soul began to wake up to see him all around me, moving and speaking and painting each day like a canvas of swirling colors. My dim and monotone world began to come alive with his pulsating movement, with the vibrant hues of God.

As light began to defy darkness, each day held more color. The orange sun radiated brighter, and I could feel the intensity of its heat on my skin more each morning. The sky shone bluer and brighter, my world humming with life and rhythm. Conversations became richer and deeper and acts of kindness drew tears to my eyes, startling me out of previous suspicion and numbness. Love began chipping away my fear, and grace whispered new mercies each morning. Hope began singing me the promise of God's closeness and redemption.

I began to experience him as a Creator God, who not only hovered over a formless and empty void at the beginning of time, but now hovered over my heart and over each day: spinning motion, weaving life, and cultivating beauty. I'm learning that there is beauty in living inside my own limits. When my days are marked with quiet, I can be more fully alive in the here and now. I see the color. Stillness and boundaries are gifts I'm still learning to receive, but when I do, I find I can approach life with more groundedness. More grace. I can more easily connect to my body, to my emotions, and to peace.

part three

CHAPTER ELEVEN

God's Whisper to the Waiting Heart

That's what anxiety did to my world: it drained the colors from life, shrouding the most basic rhythms of my daily experience in a cloudy haze. It felt suffocating, like a clenched fist had wrapped fingers around my lungs, squeezing the air out. Slowly, as this paralyzing reality consumed my life, the dreams, passions, and hopes I'd so unashamedly expressed as a little girl shriveled to the single act of existing. How can you possibly think about *dreaming* when the simple feat of breathing feels like a major undertaking? The longer anxiety clouded my world, the less I could imagine anything different.

Maybe I was just different.

But something began to happen as I carved out space for stillness and silence, and I began to learn how to be with myself and God. As I grew in awareness of my inner world and messily began reorienting my life, God drew intimately close. It was as if God himself held a fire to my soul: breathing life, rebuilding passion, and rekindling memories of little-girl Taylor who had seen color.

It was as if he was whispering into the deepest part of my being, *That's who I always created you to be.*

The more I woke up (to God, to myself, and to the inner workings of my own heart), the more I was able to glimpse a different life. An ache progressively swelled in me for a fuller and richer season. Once again, I asked God to help me understand practically what walking in freedom looks like. He continually shows me that the transformation he offers you and me encompasses far more than I imagined.

While my idea of freedom still lingered at the outermost edges of my life (physical and emotional relief from bondage), God's idea of freedom plunged much deeper into the fibers of my identity as his child. I began to realize that the shift from a slave mentality to a son-and-daughter mentality was but the beginning toward actually becoming one of his own at the core of who I am. What does this kind of freedom look like, where my deep identification as his beloved child becomes the driving force for everything I think, say, or do? The Israelites' long road back to their homeland of Canaan shows us that this journey always carries with it a sense of sacred returning. To our true name, to our deepest identity, to childlike vibrancy and dependency on the One who is writing our stories.

> At its core, the spiritual journey is one of God continually welcoming us home, not only to a truer version of him but also to a truer version of ourselves.

During this time, I spent a lot of time thinking about little-girl Taylor. That little girl, who'd splashed turquoise on paper and drew circles of emerald green, had seen the color. Words like "confident" and "grounded" and "carefree" drifted to the surface of my mind when I thought about her. That little girl wasn't afraid to receive. She lived off hope. She trusted that she would be cared for, and this truth infused her with playfulness and courage and a sense of settled conviction about her worth. But it hadn't taken long for the wounds and scars of life to teach her that colors are just for children. You can't live in the real world and survive that way.

The more she experienced the world as a frightening and unpredictable place, the more that deep and most real part of her (that tender, creative, and playful side . . . the part of her most intimately connected with her emotions) began to retreat. In its place, a hollowness settled in. A bleak sense of emptiness gradually dulled her perspective on life. Emptiness can feel so paradoxically heavy sometimes. Over time, she began the shift from living from the heart to the head, *and this journey always involves a loss of color.*

Gradually, beliefs like "God is good" and "I am accepted" and "hope is safe" and "people can be trusted" no longer became an option. While these statements had initially landed in her little-girl heart like the fluttering wings of a butterfly, the thought of them now hit her with a sickening thud. She had personal evidence against them. Personal, lived-out proof to testify against their validity in the grittiness of her story.

It didn't take long for those beliefs to give way to a harsher narrative. A grating voice that declared the anxiety-rattling story of little-girl Taylor's insufficiency. Her insufficiency to face the cruelty of life. Her insufficiency to meet the demands of a noisy and image-focused world. This voice is loud in our world today. *Not pretty enough, not good enough, not strong enough, not smart enough.* It's an experience-based teacher, at work within the external messages and subtle cues in our environment and writing into our lives a painful script of insufficiency.

The human experience was never meant to unfold this way, and in each of our healing journeys, Jesus continually invites us to a better, more truth-based story. A more truth-based perception of ourselves. There is so much more to this story than our pain often allows us to see. The freedom of God doesn't *just* usher us from a place of bondage and woundedness, but also invites us to reexperience joy. He longs to welcome us back to a place of gratitude and boldness and hope. He offers us healing that runs deeper than the "fixing" of surface-level struggles, but engages in the fundamental reordering of our minds and hearts toward a new identity—an identity intricately informed by our perception of his. He wants to resurrect wonder and hope and trust in us.

That might feel overwhelming when you read it. Maybe a little scary. It can be unnerving to even consider the possibility of allowing ourselves to hope and trust again. To actually *feel* emotions. To vulnerably lean into awe and joy without anxiously fearing we'll be blindsided by pain or disappointment. But what if we allowed ourselves to just sit and ponder what this kind of freedom might look like for us? To hold this question gently in the awakening spaces of our hearts, without having to do anything about it yet?

> For me, this healing journey first required me to untangle the messages throughout my childhood that had crafted my own "not-enough" story.

I had to trace the sequence of events, littering the stages of my development, that had caused little-girl Taylor to not feel safe to come out anymore. If these moments had caused her to slip away, then they were important to identify and understand in order for healing to begin.

Initially, my mind reverted to the catastrophic moments of life. Those defining lines in our personal histories that permanently redirected the course of our lives. That phone call, the sexual assault, the physical injury, the gaping loss, the traumatic death, that devastating emotional wound that left us raw and aching and grasping for some kind of normalcy again. Those moments often seem like they're occurring in slow motion, as if you're observing yourself from the outside. They leave a knifelike wound and stark sense inside that you won't be okay again for a long time.

But my personal "not-enough" narrative hadn't formed from these moments. Rather, I've discovered that what we come to know about ourselves is learned most powerfully *in the context of relationship.* More than the unmistakable traumas of life, this narrative took shape from the subtle social cues and micro messages saturating my childhood. These messages are much more ambiguous and can be challenging to identify. We can shame ourselves into ignoring them as unimportant and insignificant. But they mark us in profound ways.

For me, these messages sounded like: *Your value is determined by your good performance. You are not allowed to be angry or sad. There's something about you that's lacking. Something is inherently wrong with you. Attention should be avoided at all costs. It's better if you blend in. It's better if you don't have preferences. You will never fit in. You don't have what it takes to belong. You will always be on the outside.* Like stinging slivers on the surface of our hearts, they tend to go unnoticed until dozens of them fester inside us over time. They damage our sense of self-worth and heavily contribute to the distortion of color in our worlds.

To fully grasp how these messages contributed to my "not-enough" story, you have to first understand the spiritual environment I was raised in. From the time I was a little girl, I went to church every Sunday. My dad was a pastor on staff, so it's what we did. On Saturday nights, I always washed my hair for church the following morning, and I'd lay out something nicer than the clothes I'd wear on a typical Tuesday. I was often known by our congregation as the good little girl who recited verses perfectly from memory and was always polite and never complained. Although these were good, God-honoring things, some of the external messages that crept into my heart were not good. Or correct.

These messages told me that being a good Christian meant always smiling and never talking about how you really felt. I learned that putting yourself together and making sure you smelled nice is what you did before you went into God's house. Although I knew these measures were typically heeded out of respect, I noticed that other people appeared especially happy with the polished version of me. Is that how God felt about me, too?

When I was nine, my family sold our home and moved to East Asia. My parents planned to partner with local churches in efforts to advance the gospel. In the months leading up to our departure, we sold nearly everything we owned. One Saturday afternoon, I spread out all my toys, with parental instructions to choose three. Everything else ended up in a pile at our garage sale, sporting fifty-cent stickers. I didn't really know how to feel that day. It had thundered outside, so we pushed our belongings for sale under a large tent to keep them dry. I stood in the corner and watched strangers carry out our couch and kitchen table and silverware. I felt okay until a woman with short, spiky hair carried out my green bedspread. That was my new bedspread. My throat tightened with a shiver of emotion. I loved that bedspread. I loved my room. I loved my home. *I loved my life.*

I suddenly really didn't like this moment.

The losses just continued rolling in. But people kept telling me how excited I must be and how much we were honoring God by our commitment. I chalked up my grief to discontentment and determined to be fine. Wasn't it silly to be sad about toys and bed-spreads and ice-skating lessons when more important things (like gospel proclamation) were at stake? Besides, I was the good little girl who never complained. The external messages that seeped into my heart sounded something like this: Anger and sadness are not allowed. These emotions are bad. Being happy all the time is what it means to honor God.

My family moved to East Asia on Christmas Eve. We settled into a house in a suburban neighborhood surrounded by rice fields and croaking frogs. Our house was situated directly across the street from a playground, where dozens of children would congregate after school. I hadn't thought much about my physical appearance until my first day on the playground. As a Caucasian little girl wearing faded jeans and a pink t-shirt, standing among a crowd of Asian faces wearing matching school uniforms, I felt the sting of my difference for the first time.

It didn't feel good.

Over the next ten years, this harsh recognition that something is *different about me* became the recurring theme of my life. Everyone looked at me with curiosity, but few people wanted to be my friend. I understood why. I stuttered when I spoke my second language and could never quite grasp what was being said around me. The embarrassing litany of my cultural mistakes seemed to never end. It took effort to be my friend and required ceaseless patience, slow talking, and hand gesturing.

I quickly learned that although I was an interesting sight to be observed, I would never, *ever* belong. My blonde hair and blue eyes became the bane of my existence. At eleven, I remember standing in front of my bathroom mirror and seething at the white complexion staring back at me. I hated it. Everything about it. Words like "too tall" and "too white" and "too big" were the angry words that now floated to my mind when I thought about myself. I just wanted to find my place. But external messages echoed loudly in the cavernous longings of my little-girl heart, telling me that something about me was lacking. I didn't have what it took to belong. Something was inherently wrong with me.

One day, at a food court, a mentally disabled woman noticed my bright blonde hair and decided that she wanted some. She sprinted across the room and clutched a fistful of my hair, yanking it firmly and ripping it out of my head. She'd stood there next to me, holding up silky strands of gold. I don't blame her at all. She truly didn't understand what she was doing. She had merely seen something she wanted and sought to claim it. But as little-girl me held a hand to my burning scalp, a part of me curled up inside. That day, the external message had rung loud and clear: Attention should be avoided at all costs. It's not safe to come out anymore. It's far better if you disappear.

Can I hide, please? Can I be invisible?

I became determined to find a way to package myself in a more socially acceptable manner. The following day, I wound my long hair up into a bun and purchased a school uniform. I didn't go to an Asian school and certainly didn't need one. But as I stood in the dressing room, staring at my new buttoned blouse and pleated skirt, shame slithered into my story and slowly began to answer all my questions of confusion, exclusion, and uncertainty. I needed to fix myself. Something about me wasn't enough. Shame is a toxic deceiver, a betrayer of self.

> Shame misleads us into changing ourselves
> to make others feel more comfortable.

Over the last few years, I've come to understand that my school uniform symbolized more than pieces of clothing. It indicated something deeper, something connected with an internal shifting in my identity. That pleated skirt and buttoned blouse became the means by which I remade myself in order to be acceptable . . . my packaging of choice to find approval and affirmation in the eyes of others. It didn't stop there. In dozens of different ways,

I began to change myself based on the cues I was receiving from my environment.

A "packaging of self" is what many of us learn is necessary as children. As we develop and experience life in the context of our closest relationships and social circles, we learn that we are liked and accepted by constructing a version of ourselves that puts us in the most flattering light. Through the interpretation of our loudest social cues and messages, we become aware that certain things about us must change in order to meet external standards (whether explicit, implied, or self-inflicted). Our packaging is the antidote to our story of "not enough."

- We package ourselves with the clothing we wear, the haircuts we choose, the pictures we post, the cars we drive, and the houses we buy.
- We package ourselves with the words we use, the humor we employ, the parts of our personalities that we display, and the manner in which we show up in a room.
- We package ourselves through the social circles in which we are involved, the friend groups we seek, and the people and organizations we most closely identify with.
- We package ourselves through the majors we select, the careers we pursue, the activities with which we fill our time, and the churches we attend.

As we grow into adulthood, we wind more and more experiences around ourselves like bandages to camouflage our shame and make ourselves perceptible *in a way that we believe is most pleasing* to the world. The maintenance of this packaging is exhausting. It fuels the hot fires of anxiety in me. Little-girl Taylor had just wanted to belong. She was willing to do whatever it took *just to belong.* But as the colors began to fade in my world—and the further I moved from childlike trust and confidence and vibrancy—I lost sight of the God who gazed at me with love and never factored my enoughness into the equation of his acceptance for me.

The gospel proves that the very nature of our not enoughness is what compelled him toward you and me in the first place. The deepest and most natural instinct of God is to run *toward* our emptiness and lack, not away from it. This resounding truth threads itself through the pages of Scripture and is fully manifested in Christ, who wrapped himself in our skin so he could walk redemption into the darkest parts of humanity. My identity had formed apart from that narrative. I no longer defined myself by what his gaze thought about me.

Now I saw echoes of my "not enough" narrative littering my day. My anxiety about my performance. My striving to appear competent. My anxious thought process that looped around what others thought about me. My crippling anxiety whenever I felt helplessly out of control. My white-knuckled attempts to manage my world. My anxious and always "I'm fine." My overwhelming anxiety about going into a new space, with new people, especially in a new social setting. I had already written "excluded" and "not enough" and worst-case scenario into every situation.

Those echoes testified to undercurrents of shame and fear and insufficiency, pulsating through my body and consuming me with anxiety. The kind of anxiety in which my body exhibited a physiological response. Tightening my muscles and weighing on my lungs. Fueling my racing thought cycles. These echoes of "not enough" lurked on the edges of my daily experience. They felt scary to invite in, scary to process. So, I never did. Only when my pace slowed did those echoes grow louder, calling for me to acknowledge and asking for my attention.

During World War II, Erik Erikson coined a phrase that stuck: *identity crisis*. He used it to describe the disorientation of shell-shocked soldiers, returning home from war, who could not remember their names. I resonated deeply with this on the soul level. The margin that I'd slowly begun working into my days carried with it a silence that felt disorienting. Every set boundary that defeated the alluring pull of an overstuffed life felt like a declaration of resolution to the war with myself that I'd been fighting for a long time. Slowly, the haze of heart wounds began to clear. And as the static of voices (telling me all that I should be or I needed to be or wasn't) began to fade, I realized that I'd forgotten my truest name. The name of "beloved" and "child" and "chosen one" that Father God had been whispering over me from the beginning. A question that terrified me began to rise to the surface of my soul.

Who am I, really?

I had to hold space for this question. I had to learn how to sit with it, wait with it, tenderly inviting it in rather than discounting it or defaulting to external packaging. The modern word "to wait" finds its ancient roots in the active verb "to watch." This word referred to a watchman, remaining in his place at a tower to witness the occurrence of something.[1] I began to realize that, similarly, I had to remain in this place of uncertainty with patient attention. I had to linger here. I had to ask myself this question of identity and be okay with not knowing.

Slowly, I had to learn how to begin seeing myself for what I actually was and meet God there. Canadian psychologist David Benner writes, "We have to learn to see—and accept—what is really there. Stripping away our illusions is part of this process, as it reorients us toward reality. To see God as God is—not as who we want God to be—requires that we see our self as we actually are. For the same cloud of illusions obscures our view of both God and ourselves."[2] When we respond to our questions of identity with unrushed curiosity, they act like guides to a holy collision with our deepest perceptions of God. I began to sense the Spirit of God whispering a question back to me.

"But who do you say I am?" (Matt. 16:15, Mark 8:29, Luke 9:20 NLT).

Jesus asked this of the apostle Peter in many of the Gospel accounts. This is the question he gently began tilling into the ground of my heart, asking me to answer honestly. Who was God to me? My answer was found not in the rote rehearsing of head knowledge but in the untangling of my own packaging and self-perceptions. However we package ourselves, we'll always construct a counterpart, false version of God. We'll come to know a god who would create that version of ourselves, and not the One who whispers to us, "My beloved."

We must ask ourselves, "What kind of god would create the packaged version of me?" That's who our hearts know God to be, and the picture of him in which we most deeply trust. I realized that, within my story of "not enough," I had simultaneously constructed a small and insufficient god. A god who wasn't safe for me. In my anxious striving, I had constructed a god who demanded more from me than I could give. My insecurity caused me to construct a god who vacillated in his rejection and affection toward me. A god who wavered and changed and fluctuated with emotion.

But that is not the true God.

This healing journey always involves understanding our natural assumptions about God and replacing them with his own insistence of who he says he is. Because it's here, in the messy understanding of our own hearts and in the company of others on the same journey, that we can replace a fragmented knowledge of self with a restored knowledge of self in the context of our relationship with him.

CHAPTER TWELVE

Walking on Wasted Grace

Occasionally, I began to see little-girl Taylor resurface. I saw her in a silly and overembellished story I would reenact after a full day at work. I saw her in an unexpected lilt of confidence in my voice and in the rolling laughter that seemed to erupt from a deeper place inside me. The slow identification of my packaged self stirred a fresh hope that I hadn't felt in a long time. I was moving forward. I'd wake up some mornings and feel confident in keeping the waves of anxiety at bay.

Until I got triggered.

Triggers are sudden, sharp reminders of past trauma or unhealed hurt that can swoop into your day unexpectedly and spiral you into overwhelming anxiety or panic. It's that smell associated with a certain event, a familiar sound, a person, or unexpected sight that causes you to relive feelings of raw, unresolved pain. It's that sensation that results in an unanticipated wave of helplessness or lack of control. It's the picture that pops up on your screen out of nowhere or the particular social setting that fills you with inexplicable fear or shame. Suddenly, you're gasping, sweating, sensing your lungs constrict, and everyone around you is completely unaware or confused at your seemingly overblown reaction. Including you. *What is happening to me?*

In moments like these, I discovered that—quite suddenly—all this inner work and boundary setting no longer seemed relevant. Or helpful. Triggered pain immediately fires off warning signals in my brain, and before I can make sense of what is happening, my body often reacts with an upsurge of anxiety that completely severs my ability to function. No matter how hard I try to inhale, to think rational thoughts, to force peace into the chaos of my mind, my body *will not* cooperate.

Recently, I found myself in a social gathering that triggered painful memories of my sister and me on the playground, attempting to belong while wearing jeans and t-shirts among a sea of Asian faces and matching uniforms. This gathering was clearly not the same, but the social dynamics at play felt oddly familiar. Everyone else appeared connected and normal and on the inside. I felt different. Blaringly so. Although the spoken language was English, my body physically reacted with the panic and helplessness of attempting to navigate a language and cultural customs I didn't understand. Suddenly, I was small and not enough and on the outside.

I internally reverted to old coping mechanisms and responded by emotionally shutting down, not speaking, attempting to avoid attention, and trying to blend in at all costs. My anxiety felt so overwhelming that it was difficult to form a coherent thought, let alone naturally engage in the conversation at hand.

My powerlessness to control these physiological responses often throws me into a tailspin of shame and frustration. Why did it seem like I'd just taken a hundred steps backward? Although I am healing, parts of me are still tender and quick to run from exposure. Whenever a painful memory is triggered or my felt sense of safety is threatened, I often find myself subconsciously slipping into the roles again, immediately reverting into the familiarity of my packaging. It can feel *nearly impossible* to pull truth in these moments.

To the anxious soul, packaging can often feel like a paradoxical dilemma. It buries the little girl inside us, severing joy and hindering authenticity, but it also keeps her safe. And anxiety is all about the maintenance of a felt sense of safety. Anxiety can masquerade as an inner voice of caution, urging me to hide behind my packaging to escape the unpredictable nature of reality. It constructs in me an inner rigidity that becomes the tight and narrow avenues through which I engage in life. The anxious life is oriented around stiff beliefs and safety behaviors that smell like control but are merely the illusion of it. It is one of precaution and overthinking and avoidance. The tight interior spaces in which anxiety tells me to abide feel like protection but lead to a life of hiding and panicked inflexibility and smallness.

Those rooted beliefs were displayed most transparently when I got triggered, and when my body physiologically swung into a fight-or-flight response. *Danger!* The power of a trigger is in the story it tells me: *Right now, you are on your own. You must keep yourself safe.* There were obvious physiological components at play. Our lungs often interpret our brain's flight-or-flight response as a loss of oxygen (and the inability to get enough), which spikes panic and anxiety. But deeper undercurrents were also heightened during these moments, circulating in my thoughts and internally screaming that I was alone and the only person I could truly depend on was *me*.

I began to realize that my packaging wasn't merely my way of presenting myself as acceptable to the world, but a safety behavior I clung to in moments of panic or uncertainty. When I was triggered, I used my packaging to cope. Trying to appear perfect. Doing anything to please and fiercely avoiding displeasure. Avoiding attention at all costs. Attempting to blend in to my surroundings. These were my ways of maintaining a sense of control and avoiding exposure. I never showed up *in my anxiety*. I never invited anyone into it. I always sought to cover it up.

Anxiety looks like clenched fists, white-knuckled grips, tight shoulders, and tense muscles. The posture I often reverted to was self-protective, arms wrapped around my body. These physical postures of tightness and confinement mirrored the deeper spaces of my soul. I feared any kind of open posture, physically or spiritually. Too vulnerable. I needed to figure out an exit route, leading to a place where the air wasn't so thin. I needed to figure out how to make the danger go away. I needed to fix this situation right now. It was all on me. It could only be on me.

> The version of God with whom I was most acquainted was too small to see me in my insufficiency and meet me in my need.

During my time in treatment, I'd often doodle the words *grace upon grace* on the corners of journal pages and pen those words in black ink across my forearm. Later, I even painted the phrase on a piece of pottery that I positioned on the nightstand in my bedroom. I'd lie awake at night and stare at those words. What does it mean to receive grace? To live in it? To be drenched in it? My struggles with anxiety and anorexia had long since suffocated any sense of grace in my life. Grace was a concept I couldn't understand or comprehend. But I wanted to.

As I began to unpack the many layers of my packaging and trace the deeper story to triggering moments (our triggers always have their origins in painful or traumatic experiences), my vision began to clear. I began to realize that my packaging hadn't merely distorted my concept of both myself and God, but had deadened my responsiveness to grace. And our movement forward on this journey is *inseparably connected* with our openhandedness toward grace.

Grace is the active expression of the love of God, the outpouring of his heart, rushing into our souls at the smallest opening of clenched fists. It is the tangible manifestation of the Father's pursuit of our own healing. Psychiatrist and theologian Gerald G. May writes that "grace is the most powerful force in the universe. It can transcend repression, addiction, and every other internal or external power that seeks to oppress the freedom of the human heart. Grace is where our hope lies."[1]

The grace of God resounds not just at salvation but *every moment of our lives*, longing to cultivate an inner space of safety that is independent from anything going on in our external environment, where we can rest. When I participate with grace, my not enoughness is flooded with his more than enoughness. No matter how physiologically triggering a situation may seem, grace helps me see these moments in the light of reality: tenderly and sovereignly controlled by a loving God. I'm reminded that whatever I face, I never face it alone. I am never on my own. I am never stuck with whatever I can muster in my own strength. I have access to resources beyond myself that always exist, are always accessible, and never run out.

Grace hovers over our packaged selves, but it won't enter unless it's invited. It seeks out those deeper places in us, longing to heal, to hold, and to make whole. But for so long, grace had merely inhabited the fringes of my packaged self. Dozens of scribbled notebook pages testified to my awareness of grace, but my inability to invite it deeply into my life. Self-deception had strangled my capacity to receive it. I felt trapped outside of grace. My packaging had allowed me to deny my not enoughness, but in doing so, had invalidated my need for grace. All that packaging simply attested to the years I'd spent proving I didn't need it.

For me, receiving grace meant facing the core fear that had caused me to hide behind my packaging in the first place: *I am not enough.* That was painful to do. I'd grown comfortable inside the structures and confines that anxiety had built in me, doubting if anything would hold me up if I truly let go. The risk of receiving, and the exposure that this position required of me, had resulted in a different kind of emptiness. A void where grace was waiting to flow in and fashion something new.

The invitation that grace extends toward me and you is not simply to erect more safety structures through a spiritual lens, but to follow Jesus in a process that leads us to a spaciousness that characterizes true freedom. To less solid edges. Less emphasis on rigidity and rule keeping and safety measures. Less clutching and grasping and finagling for control. Less white-knuckled approach to life. Less compulsive need for predictability. In this process, we are led in the direction of unconditional love, *where fear has no place.* We find ourselves steadied on a soft foundation where we can take risks, make mistakes, and try new things, all while being held securely. This is the offering of grace: to become so grounded in the loving gaze of Christ that we can live out the truth of our neediness without fear or shame.

Most days, it's still hard for me to understand this kind of freedom fully. How do I even begin to let go that completely? I long for the inner spaciousness that Jesus promises us, but I fear opening up, releasing those safety structures that have become subconsciously rhythmic for me, and engaging in life without them. This means when my knees buckle under me, I don't fall back into rigidity, but I fall back into grace. And grace operates fluidly, beyond the bounds of my sense of control, filling me with a conflicting tension between freedom and familiarity.

> Grace is our empowerment to let go of familiarity and walk out something new; however, the spaciousness of freedom can feel at first like caverns of loss.

There is a man in Scripture who I believe understood this tension between freedom and familiarity. His story is recorded in Luke 7, where he interacts with Jesus personally over a meal at his table. The fact that Jesus is found at his home surprises many biblical scholars, as Simon was a Pharisee. And Pharisees rarely invited Jesus into their private, inner space. Pharisees were the religious leaders of Jesus's day, known for upholding 613 commandments extraneously interpreted from the law of Moses. The life of a Pharisee was oriented around customary props and rule-keeping, which they observed with careful rigidity. Their way of life is commonly perceived as hypocritical and purposefully contrary to the way of Jesus, but I've often wondered what truly sat behind their thinking and responses.

Could fear, rather than defiance, have been the strongest motivator of their hearts? What if at the core of their structured lifestyle was a frantic grasping for security? *If I just stay within these set structures, I will be safe. I will be seen how I want to be seen.* To some extent, isn't this the mind-set we all have? The more I study these men, the more I see a deeper vein of misguided sincerity. I see anxious hearts, steeped in habitual familiarity. I see a fierce allegiance to what was known and a deep-seated fear of the unknown. Which would have included the controversial teachings of Jesus.

During this same time, Jesus was offering up a new and radical lifestyle to his listeners. One defined by grace, which went against the grain of everything these Pharisees had built their lives around. This new way of life involved the demolishing of safety structures for a deeper kind of openhandedness. Less upkeeping of old routines and more release into an entirely new way of being. To the anxious soul, old routine can feel like the better option if it keeps those safety structures close. *I resonate with this deeply.* Those two paths form the crossroad between familiarity and freedom. At this crossroad, we are met with the question of whether or not we will open ourselves up to the floodgates of grace. We can't walk our freedom without it.

In Luke 7, we see this inner tension welling up inside Simon during Jesus's visit to his home. He appears hardened and cynical toward Jesus. Resistant against this man sitting across from him, who embodies a lifestyle contrary to anything he has ever known. As they sit and eat together, a prostitute comes in and kneels beside Jesus. Weeping, she begins kissing his feet and drying them with her tears. You can almost feel Simon seething. This woman's honest display of the most hidden and not-yet-healed parts of herself represents everything unsafe and inappropriate to him. She comes to Jesus publicly, stripped of external packaging, and freely invites grace into these messy, interior spaces.

I can only imagine the offended expression on Simon's face. This woman, in all her flagrant deficiency, would have been judged severely by the Pharisees, her actions toward Jesus viewed as shameful. An offense. But she was not despised by Jesus. As Simon watched Jesus sit unhurriedly with brokenness and saturate her not enoughness with his mercy-rich heart, I wonder what he was thinking. Did he feel the difference between this woman and himself? The distance between him and this shame-obliterating wave of grace? Jesus's response toward Simon captivates me. It's as if Jesus sees his shock and quick offense and capitalizes on the moment, gently engaging him in conversation about this unfolding scene. His words unpack for me the nuances of grace in our healing journeys.

While Simon had not offered Jesus water to wash his feet, Jesus says, this woman washed the dust off his feet with her tears. While Simon had not offered Jesus the customary kiss of greeting, this woman had yet to stop kissing his feet. While Simon had not anointed Jesus with oil, this woman poured perfume over his head. These comparisons jarred Simon of everything he'd learned to place his trust in.

The prostitute and the Pharisee. They both had debts. But it was the prostitute on her knees, not the Pharisee who immersed himself in his old routines, who had received grace. Jesus's deeper meaning, layered with invitation, is clear. *Oh, Simon. You haven't truly welcomed me in. Stop proving and performing and bring your mess to me. Invite me in . . . all the way in . . . and let my grace flow freely.* That was the invitation of Jesus to Simon, and that is his invitation to you and me. *Come to me in your need*, he says. *Come and let me love you.*

The Pharisee represents that psychological substructure inside us, manifested in anxious rigidity and habitual routine, that at its core lacks felt awareness of the love of Christ. This story shows us that—deeper than the effects of trauma, the scars of childhood wounds, and the external messages that have shaped how we see and engage in life—there exists an incomplete picture of *his unrestrained grace.*

The One to whom all of heaven ceaselessly cries "Holy, Holy, Holy" is also the One who bore a bloodied cross for us. He is the One whose anguish (translated as "anxiety" in Greek) was so overwhelming in the garden of Gethsemane that he sweated blood. Both invincibly victorious and intimately acquainted with our hearts, he promises to soothe, sustain, strengthen, and experientially walk through our anxiety *with us.* But we must come to him like the woman in Luke 7: inviting him in, open to truth, and needy for grace.

As this prostitute beautifully depicts, there is a loving release that precedes this deeper ushering in of grace into our lives. A releasing of old routines that had once promised to keep us safe. We must replace our packaging with a posture that showcases the full-blown reality of our not enoughness. Stripped of safety behaviors and in touch with the sharp reality of our insufficiency, we come face-to-face with the grace of Christ. Here, the words of David in Psalm 51 resound: "For the source of your pleasure is not in my performance or the sacrifices I might offer to you. The fountain of your pleasure is found in the sacrifice of my shattered heart before you. You will not despise my tenderness as I bow down humbly at your feet" (Ps. 51:16–17 TPT).

> Grace most longs to move in to the
> fractures of the shattered heart.

I had watched the movie *The Passion of the Christ* a few days before visiting the bustling streets of Jerusalem, so the morning that my study group walked the Via Dolorosa (the road where Christ carried his cross), the movie's vivid scenes depicting his suffering on the same road weighed heavily. This narrow alley where he had shouldered a splintered cross held a sacredness that's difficult to articulate. He had been carrying my cross. Your cross. The black and ugly magnitude of a sinful, suffering world. And now I walked on the same road this bright Tuesday morning, light and free. It was as if my shoulders physically felt the lifted weight.

Certain locations on the Via Dolorosa indicate significant historical occurrences on the day of Jesus's crucifixion, and our guide was quick to reference several numerically marked posts as we walked. We paused at the place where Jesus had stood before

Pontius Pilate, and we lingered at the space where Jesus would have been flogged. I felt tears fill my eyes as I imagined the jeering mob, the glazed eyes of his accusers, the thorns plunged through his scalp, and the shredded skin of his back. In each of these locations, scenes from the movie played in my mind and allowed me to relive the day as if I was actually experiencing it. After we had walked for a few moments, we reached the marked location where Mary is historically described as comforting Jesus when he falls under the weight of the cross.

I vividly recalled this scene.

As we stood, a sobering silence rippling through our small study group, I thought about Mary on that day, and in this moment. What might she have been feeling? Did she understand the weight of his sacrifice? I can only imagine the memories flooding her mind of Jesus playing and laughing as a child. Had she seen this day coming? When Jesus stumbles, *The Passion of the Christ* portrays Mary hunched over him, weeping. For the briefest of moments, Jesus looks up at her and whispers softly into her ear, "I have come to make *all things* new." As their eyes lock, her heart stirs with understanding: *that included her, too.*

Suddenly, their roles are reversed. The mother in her becomes a child at the feet of her Maker, recognizing the depths of her weakness, the power of his grace, and the price of both.[2] Another scene depicts her kneeling in the courtyard where Jesus was flogged, wiping up pools of his blood. On a personal level, her eyes had opened to his costly sacrifice, *and it's as if she doesn't want to waste one drop of the blood.*

This was and always is supposed to be our response to grace. I've never been entirely against grace, but most of my life has consisted of just letting it trickle in through the cracks of my packaged self. I've struggled to understand it and to step into my need for it. As if the grace of God was in short supply, I viewed it as something that was given to me in droplets of faltering resignation and not the gushing, magnanimous grace that knows no limit . . . spilling as freely from his heart today as his freely shed blood on the cross.

I don't want to waste this grace. I want to receive this outpouring of love, letting it flood every part of my life. I want to cooperate with this work of Christ that continually meets us right where we are, yet always calls us forward. I discount the sacrifice of Jesus when I don't think I need it and when I fail to receive it as the gift that it is.

As we open our hands to grace, allowing it to sweep away our stiff beliefs and safety behaviors, how does this transform our anxiety? How does grace change the way we breathe and physiologically respond to triggering moments and anxiety-marked days? I can't help but think back on Jesus's crucifixion, where, on reaching the end of this road, he was nailed to a cross, arms stretched out and open. What a vulnerable and dangerous place to be. And yet, there was this groundedness about Jesus, this sense of settled belief, that allowed him to launch into this moment fully aware of the end result, and yet knowing at his core that the Father's tender gaze was fixed on him. And that he was seen and securely held, even in a space *that felt everything but that.*[3] He opened himself up and stretched himself out without hesitation, knowing that he was safe.

What if this is what healing looks like, on a spiritual, emotional, and even physiological level? As we inhale the grace of God's unconditional love and let it touch our innermost parts, we're able to release tense muscles and straighten hunched shoulders, adhering closer and closer to the posture of our crucified Christ. Slowly, we begin to live stretched out and open, knowing the Father's gaze is fixed on us and we are safe. *Even in spaces that feel anything but that.*

After returning home from Israel, I began drawing a cross on my wrist. Two black swooshes across pale skin, right where my faded eating disorder henna used to be. Words from the psalmist echoed in my spirit: "God, you're such a safe and powerful place to find refuge! You're a proven help in time of trouble—*more than enough* and always available whenever I need you. So we will never fear even if every structure of support were to crumble away" (Ps. 46:1–2 TPT—emphasis in original).

Oh, Jesus. Help me to see you as my safe place, my more-than-enough God, even if every structure of support were to crumble away. Especially when every structure of support crumbles away. The more I release my need to be enough, the more I am able to breathe and rest in a deeper place of safety. I've found that in this place where I'd anxiously feared a free fall, I was already being held in the gentle arms of grace.

CHAPTER THIRTEEN

Coexisting with Uncertainty

The uncertainty of walking through hardship without knowing the outcome often feels like more than I can handle. My confusion and angst can send me on a hard search for the tidy lesson, the quick solution, so I can fit all this pain into my fragile grasp of who I know God to be. I search tirelessly for the hidden sin or easy explanation that, if identified, will transform my situation instantaneously. What is the purpose of my pain? Maybe if I figure out what God is trying to teach me, I can move on faster. My tendency is to reconcile his goodness by imagining *and trusting in* a fairy-tale ending that he never promised me. Then I get angry and offended when it doesn't turn out as I envisioned.

Many of us live scared of uncertainty. The uncertainty in our relationships, our health, our futures. However, an integral part of healing from anxiety is learning how to coexist with such uncertainties. We've often been taught to box the doubts and quiet questions of our lives, as if our certainty about everything is indicative of our belief. Empty platitudes become the white noise that drowns the inner cacophonies of our silent questions.

"God won't give you more than you can handle."

"Let go and let God."

"You just need to pray more."

We don't know how to respond to pain that lingers or suffering that persists despite our prayers for the opposite. Although I don't believe we should ever stop believing and praying for change, how often do our prayers sound more like personalized escape plans than a "not my will but your will be done"? In the face of unforeseen pain and lasting struggles, how often do we write our own exit strategies and label *that* faith?

We write a better and more black-and-white ending, according to us, and then hold God to accomplishing our plan. Although we testify to the sufficiency of God's grace and power in our weakness, the truth is we aren't comfortable with the actual manifestation of it. But when we deny our own finiteness and fragility, refusing to acknowledge them as an expected reality, we don't have language to process our pain. We don't have words to name our wounds or the vocabulary to reach for healing. Silence strips us of our ability to receive empathy, connection, or grace. We become fixated on an outcome. Our capacity to hope is tied to happy endings and not to the God who holds us securely in our falling apart.

Suffering disorients us on the soul level. When we criticize or distance ourselves from our emotions, we begin to lose our sense of where we are. Detaching from our experiences prevents us from inviting God's presence into the reality of our pain. Our spiritual and secular environments often resound with the same message: *pretend like you're fine.* This external pressure has shaped many of our inner dialogues in response to suffering. Deny that something feels off inside. Invalidate the uncertainty. Pull yourself together. Move on faster. Spin a shinier ending. We must defy the subtle but pervading belief that pretending will eventually result in healing. When we attempt to rush past or hide our pain, we stop inhabiting our lives. Living ahead of the present moment, we don't experience God in the places where we need him the most.

> To trust that God is truly good is to hold his self-proclaimed goodness in one hand and the reality of my pain in the other, and for there to be no competition between the two.

I'm not there yet. My anxiety spirals in the face of uncertainty. I feel the tension of my unanswered questions in the presence of an all-knowing God. I seek comfort in knowing all the answers and all the reasons. The ambiguity of throbbing questions and blurred lines makes me feel completely out of control. Today, my mind travels to the situations in my life that feel unstable and complicated. If I dwell here too long, my sense of helplessness morphs into anxiety and anger at God. *Why don't you fix it? Why aren't you intervening? Where are you when I need you? Why are you being silent?*

He responds with a quiet reminder of his presence.

The longer I've walked this inward journey, the more that grace has painted the truth of who God really is. No longer do I see him as a distant and disapproving god who fills me with fear. As old versions of him are put to death, I've encountered a God who promises to meet me *in my fear*. With transformed sight, I've begun to see the compassion of God and the depths of his affection for me. He is the embodiment of everything beautiful and good and true, Love incarnate, moving into the messiest parts of my life and making his home there.

This God is the opposite of how I thought he was supposed to work and far different from anything I'd envisioned him to be.

Rather than answering my prayers to instantaneously fix me or my situation, this God continually promises to conjoin his heart to mine as a cosufferer. He works in ways beyond my understanding and chooses to feel my pain in ways he doesn't have to. More than giving me all the answers to my questions, he sits with me in the unknown. He holds me through anxiety rather than immediately rescuing me from it. And instead of hurrying to make my struggles past tense, he is always inviting me into greater honesty with him about it.

The version of God that I had crafted would rescue me from my problems if he truly loved me. He would have stopped the pain and trauma. He would have reverted the trajectory of my life away from bathroom-floor moments well before I reached that point. If God was truly good, I would never wonder why he sometimes seemed to go silent. But these godlike qualities smell synthetic and shallow. They don't reflect the mystery of this crucified Christ who personally chose a path of suffering himself, and who promised to stand with me in the breaking rather than always sparing me from it. He continually shows himself as a God of patience, working most frequently in slow processes and unseen purposes.

God's definition of goodness is clearly different than mine. While my default is to define goodness as the absence of pain, he defines goodness as the steadfastness of his presence. This continually leaves a rift inside me between believing the love of God and feeling that it is true. How does the goodness and kindness of God manifest itself in suffering? Have you felt this tension, too? It's relatively easy to reconcile an uncaring god with the brokenness of our stories. All the pain and uncertainty pervading our lives is appropriately put in context. It's much harder to reconcile a God who insists on his love and presence when the circumstances of our lives don't seem to attest to this truth.

The challenge for me is to trust God's goodness when he works in ways I don't understand. To rest in his hidden purpose when I don't see it and to allow his will in my life when his voice seems to go silent. I feel hurt and ask him questions like, *What? Why? Where are you? Can you explain what you're doing?* I'm discovering that I need to relearn how to know God in hardship.

As my heart continues to align with a truer version of God, and as slow healing progressively seeps into my life, I've found that my questions have begun to change in nature. The more I experience the love of God and the reality of his all-consuming grace, the less I question the fact of his goodness. And the more I ask him to teach me how to trust him when I don't see it. *Oh, Jesus.* How do I stay emotionally regulated and spiritually grounded in uncertainty? Will you teach me how to know I am held by you, even in all my messiness and fighting and pain?

During my sophomore year of high school, I spent a week volunteering at an orphanage in Southeast Asia. Located in a small and impoverished city of bustling streets and thickly polluted air, this place felt special from the moment our old bus clattered down the driveway. The building's bright blue and green exterior, fringed with painted trees and flowers, sharply contrasted the monotone grayness of the city. It was quiet here. Almost eerily so. Although the rooms of this orphanage housed the neglected and abandoned, its unsoiled floors and sterile halls didn't reflect the normal grime and wear of a bustling children's home. Its empty halls echoed, void of pattering feet and laughter.

All 144 occupants of this orphanage were either permanently handicapped or terminally ill.

That is why this brightly painted and uniquely purposed orphanage existed: for the forgotten of society, the lowest of the low. Those little ones with the life slowly draining from them spent their days laying quietly on mats of freshly washed linens, their illnesses taking the shape of large cancerous lumps on their bodies or the rigid limbs of cerebral palsy. Time passed slowly as we moved from room to room, cradling infants and sitting with the tiny, fragile bodies of the dying. Our work felt small but was threaded with the sacred. It was as if the space between heaven and earth had grown thin here.

As a sixteen-year-old walking these halls, I knew I'd already lived years beyond what most of these children would ever experience. That reality rattled me. On Sunday mornings sitting in church pews, I was consistently assured of God's miracle-working power and immeasurable goodness. But what was I supposed to do with that information on a Tuesday afternoon, sitting in a house like this, full of suffering children who he wasn't healing? Where was his goodness? The pain and death housed within those four walls cut deep, carving away layers of the Sunday school version of Jesus I'd been taught as a child. That picture-book version of a divinity who blessed the little children in no way seemed to reflect my current experience.

A few years later, this growing sense of uncertainty became deeply personal as I wrestled with my own worsening sickness. As my family navigated some significant changes while in the throes of another cross-cultural transition, unanticipated struggles and future uncertainties seemed to spiral without an end in sight. *God, heal me. Help me. Please intervene.* I prayed those prayers over and over again. The sicker I grew, the more numb I became to hope. I watched him work out healing and happy endings in the lives of others that seemed to skip me. I'd often curl up in a tight ball at night, swallowing mouthfuls of unspoken questions. God's goodness seemed cruelly distant from the stark reality of my pain. My mind often wandered back to that week in the orphanage. One evening in particular continued to surface.

The sunset had been especially beautiful that night, so after a late dinner of steamed rice and stir-fried pork and vegetables in the kitchen adjoining our bedrooms, I'd escaped upstairs to the rooftop terrace for a breath of fresh air. Journal flipped open and untouched, I'd sat at an empty picnic table, watching the amber glow of the sun sink beneath the dusty city skyline. A lone staff member hunched over a bed of potted plants, watering seeds and pulling weeds. As I slowly scanned my surrounding, my gaze caught on one of the walls nearest to me. It had been covered with names.

Shadows crept across the terrace as I meandered over to the wall, running my fingers across the rough concrete. The staff member's voice sliced the silence, her broken English piecing together meaning: "Those are the new names of all the children who have died here, written by their individual caregivers." Penned in pinks and purples and greens, each name bore its own unique font. I touched the names, one by one, thinking about that little life. This wall stood in sharp contrast to my own outlook on pain and suffering.

Hide it. Disguise it. Keep it like a secret.

As I looked at this wall, I saw blatantly visible that, in this place, the brokenness invading their short existences wasn't seen as a secret to be concealed but an honor to be remembered. A symbol of hope. This wall wasn't hidden but on display for everyone to see. These brightly penned names had transformed a simple, concrete slab into something strikingly beautiful. I thought about the big, bold letters on the sign in the front yard and all the brochures stuffed in logoed envelopes on the first floor. This place of death had been renamed a "House of Hope."

Inside these walls, names were written in the cyclical wake of reoccurring death and devastating endings. Death wasn't the end but the birthing of a new identity. Here, suffering wasn't viewed as a source of shame but of stewardship. As I think back on that evening, I can't help but wonder. *Is that how it was always supposed to be?* I'd been told a hundred times that God was a redemptive God, intent on creating beauty. He is good, his ways are good, and he always promises to lead us down good paths.

> But maybe his goodness has never been about removing pain but renaming it.

That truth, like a seed, continues to work itself out in my life. My default has always been to view suffering as a detour to the good life that God intended for me. Bathroom-floor moments were temporary delays, and hardship a thing to be conquered to move on to better things. My finite understanding of a good God would quickly dissolve hardship from my life, always leading me on paths away from pain. And if he didn't? Maybe something was wrong with me. I must have strayed off course somehow. Or perhaps he wasn't who he said he was.

But when we look at Jesus, we see the embodiment of goodness himself choosing to enter the human story *to suffer.* He was a man of many sorrows. One who was well acquainted with grief (Isa. 53:3 NLT). In Scripture, we see a God who wept and grew weary and willingly bled. To him, suffering wasn't a problem to escape but a path to be stewarded. In the good story that God was weaving throughout history, he chose to use the broken body of his Son to shape our brokenness into something beautiful. His self-sacrifice was the catalyst for hope to be unleashed. I can't see any beauty in crucifixion. I don't see any goodness in it at all. But to our God, the sight of his crucified Son was the most beautiful sight of all. The scars that mark his resurrected body give shape to what grace looks like.

These translucent pages continually testify to a God who never avoided pain himself and *never* promised to keep us from it. But he always promised to meet us in our brokenness and to call us his beloved. Jesus's scars speak to this truth. His earthly call hadn't been to escape suffering but to live out the truth of his belovedness through his suffering. Could the same be true for us?

> Maybe healing isn't about the absence of scars but an alignment of the heart toward an identity that runs deeper than our woundedness.

It's always in those moments when I'm brought to the edge of myself, bringing my hurts, fears, and questions into the open and right up to his face, that I realize his loving gaze has never left me. And the more I allow the chaos of my heart to clash against the unchanging features of his, the more I leave knowing that I am truly his beloved. Nothing will change that. Nothing has and nothing will.

Jacob is a biblical character found in the Old Testament who understood this paradox well. Unhealed wounds and relational tension are threaded throughout his story. He spent the first decades of his life attempting to escape pain and distance himself from uncertainty. On a night when Jacob was alone, after having done everything possible to secure his own safety, he meets God. Genesis 32 records a wrestling match between Jacob and God, *which God initiates.* This passage speaks to a shifting in Jacob's identity as he comes to a sharper knowledge of his own finiteness and is awakened to the power and presence of God. During the wrestling God renamed Jacob "Israel." Jacob leaves this encounter with God transformed and permanently marked by the reality of his weakness and God's strength.

We are each called to fully indwell the story we've been given, being present in every moment. The joy, the grief, and the longings. Rather than straining to see a future outcome, God continually calls us into a deeper awareness of today. Right here in the middle of the unknown, midstory, in the messy unfolding of that circumstance far from our choosing. Acknowledging our fears and paying attention to our own hearts in the presence of the love and compassion of God is how we live with uncertainty. We must be honest with him. Fiercely so. Honesty is what keeps us rooted, both creating and nourishing intimacy.

Maybe suffering isn't a hindrance to goodness. When I revisit my story, I see that suffering in the hands of God has become a tool of transforming grace *that is shaping goodness in me.* Maybe the script that suffering writes in my life was never intended to falsely rename God but to more truthfully rename *me.* Through pain and death, our new name is being birthed in us. As I'm learning how to coexist with uncertainty, I'm discovering God is big enough to handle my doubts, my fears, and my questions. My uncertainty doesn't need to drive me away from God. Rather, my uncertainties can actually become pathways leading me deeper into him. More often than not, it's in these very places of wrestling that Love is remaking me, doing its best and most transformative work, and whispering to me the names of my deepest identity.

CHAPTER FOURTEEN

Becoming the Beloved

I've always wanted that miraculous deliverance moment when I would never feel the air-sucking, claustrophobic feeling of anxiety again. I've prayed for the fast cure. The ten-step guarantee where the darkness leaves and the destructive patterns disappear and the panic dissipates for peace. But that has not been my story.

Over the last five years, I've spent thousands of hours in quiet places with the Spirit of God, in the company of professional counselors, and within the community of Christ: digging into my own heart, encountering the God that indwells me. Although I still struggle with anxiety, I'm thankful that I'm healing. *Really healing.* The inner work required for this kind of walk isn't easy. It can be jarring. Messy. Complicated. But it brings about deep and meaningful transformation in every single part of our lives. On this road, we become more and more awake to beauty. We begin to see the dim outline of what a life shaped by love, rather than fear, might look like.

Along this journey, we must *move toward* our anxiety to move through it. That's what we've begun to do together in these pages. We've moved toward the fears. Toward the hurt. Toward the pain in our stories, and all lies underneath. As we do, we move toward God.

Our lives can be filled with so much chaos and dysfunction, dragging us away from the inner quiet place where Love lives. Our world often feels overstimulating at times, radiating with information and assumptions and opinions that scream for our attention and grasp for a role in our formation. Telling us who we are or who we should be or who we need to be in order to belong. All too quickly, I get ungrounded. I get triggered. And all that noise unsteadies me, causing me to lose my emotional footing and sense of stability. Flustered, I lose my capacity to control the spiraling thoughts, the damp palms and tightened muscles, the foggy brain and fragmented nerves. I begin the spiraling nose dive into not enough.

I have to keep returning to and trusting the truth that even when I feel utterly weak and alone, God is with me. He continually invites me to untangle myself from all that noise and fully inhabit today. Only as I've practiced being present in the here and now, slowly opening myself up to the full truth of my story, have I begun to experience the peace that can exist beneath the chaos. Again and again, I have to get out that black pen and draw truth over what feels like a thousand invisible reminders of my lack. That ink-smudged cross on my wrist testifies to the blood of Jesus covering me: *By his wounds, I am healed. His power is made perfect in my weakness. His grace is sufficient for me* (see Isa. 53:5; 2 Cor. 12:9).

In a small garden chapel in Jerusalem, I recently sat on a hard-backed pew and took communion. This time I stayed in my seat, holding the tiny, goblet-shaped cup and wafer in an open palm.

Sunlight slanted in through stained-glass windows, chasing away shadows. Years had passed since I'd sunk numbly into another church pew. I'd felt like a vacant shell, the bread and the cup but stale reminders of healing and wholeness unavailable to me. I remembered my pleas as I begged God to fix me.

He'd felt coldly silent.

I'd gotten up and left the room.

Here I sat five years later, once again holding these sacred symbols. I still wasn't fixed. At least, not in the way I had wanted. Not in the way that I'd prayed for. But where I had asked for the power that delivered, I had received the grace that sustained. A soft breeze danced as I listened to rich vibrato recite words from the apostle Paul: "Whenever you eat this bread and drink this cup, you are retelling the story, proclaiming our Lord's death until he comes" (1 Cor. 11:26 TPT). I chewed the bread and lifted the cup to my lips, tilting my chin. Red liquid spilled as I swallowed. I thought about his blood, running from a crown of gnarled thorns.

> As I retold his story, the Spirit of God whispered that he is retelling mine.

What a cup of suffering Jesus drank for you and me. No hesitation. No second-guessing. Not a split second of doubt. As he poured out his life on the cross, he stamped victory over my story. With one decisive act, he'd forever stripped darkness of its power, dispensing the fullness of his life into the frailty of mine. I exhaled, settling into the truth that I could truly trust him. Whether healing came through the sudden work of his power or the steady work of his presence, I wasn't alone. I was never abandoned. And whatever he chose to not remove from my life, he would give me the grace to drink it.

And he would drink it with me.

The pungent aftertaste of grapes lingered on my tongue as I thought back to the night Jesus had been arrested. Scripture recounts that, after eating the Passover meal with his disciples and sharing in communion with them, he'd begun walking a worn path toward a small garden at the foot of the Mount of Olives. The garden of Gethsemane. Jesus speaks some of his final words to those closest to him in these last moments together. He knew the darkness of the world, keenly aware of the darkness at work that night. He knew what lay ahead for each of these men, intimately acquainted with every moment of their stories. He knew their weaknesses and wounds. He was mindful of their fears and flaws and inadequacies.

"I love each of you with the same love that the Father loves me," he spoke into that murky night, whispering truth over rattled hearts. I imagine tenderness in his eyes. "You must remain in life-union with me, for I remain in life-union with you." His last words hadn't been a rallying of strength and audacious bravado, but rather a call to remember their need: "You must continually let my love nourish your hearts" (John 15:9, 4 TPT).

He didn't tell them to stop being afraid.

He called them to know that they are loved.

Silence permeated that small, sunlit chapel. For years, anxiety had gutted me of the felt love of Christ. I'd scurried to get fixed, entangled by insecurity and shame. Where's the loophole to this process? Where's the part of this story where I finally stop struggling? I'd sung that familiar line, "Oh, how sweet to trust in Jesus," inside the walls of our churches more times than I could count. But the truth was I'd fiercely mistrusted the words that Love has spoken over me. Fusing victory with tidy endings, I've left little space for the not-yet-healed and still-broken parts of me to receive grace. I've been dead set on not being the weak one.

I wanted to be the courageous overcomer. Then maybe I would feel that I was loved.

> But Jesus invites me to be the broken one who knows that I am his beloved today.

Much of this book has unpacked the truth that God sees us and loves us in our darkest moments. He is our cosufferer. He's the God who hunches low on the floor with us, enveloping our shame in a rushing undercurrent of undeserved grace. He's not a distant God, removed from our pain. I think about the night that Jesus would be arrested, when soon after speaking those words to his disciples, emotional anguish twisted so intensely inside him that he sweated drops of blood. This nail-scarred God is the One who extends the invitation to intimacy; this God who could have protected himself from agony but didn't. Rather, he chose to enter into the thick of the human experience, testifying that he empathizes with us. He feels. He understands. And he invites us to let that truth become our vision, our testimony, our hope, and our deepest consolation.

The apostle Peter was one of the disciples in the garden of Gethsemane that night, sensing the confusion and heaviness of the moment. Just a few hours later, he was also the one who stood around a coal-lit fire, and when asked if he knew Jesus, he denied it three times. Panic drove Peter into a deep vault of self-protection. He'd slid into survival mode, terrified of being discovered. *I know that place well.*

I imagine Peter had never envisioned he'd see Jesus here. The last time he'd caught a glimpse of Jesus, he'd been roughly thrust into Caiaphas's house, shackled and bound. Peter watched his completely sovereign Messiah remain silent, refusing to utter a syllable in protest. It must have made no sense to him. With an icy gust of wind, I imagine he must have felt a deeper shiver of lostness. A sense of disorientation on the soul level. Where had Jesus gone?

Tradition recounts Peter lingering on a deck outside Caiaphas's house when this brief moment occurred. I've stood on that deck in Jerusalem, gazing at the ancient ruins of the staircase leading into the city, where Jesus walked just moments after Peter's denial. It was here that Jesus most likely paused as he shuffled downward, locked in the skin-chafing iron of Roman chains. As Peter watched from the courtyard, warming his frozen hands over a crackling fire, Jesus *turned and looked straight at him* (Luke 22:61 NIV).

I've always wondered about the look in Jesus's eyes. If I had been Peter, I would have anticipated condemnation and disappointment written all over his face. But when peeling back the word "look" to the original language, the Greek word here is *emblepo*, which can be translated as an intense gaze of love, interest, or concern.[1]

I knew that look. I'd seen it in the eyes of G as we walked to the clinic on that frozen March morning. I'd seen it in the eyes of S as I sat in his office, hiding beneath layers of knitted wool. I'd seen it in the eyes of my dad as he hoisted my suitcase from the trunk of our rental car parked in front of my treatment facility. I'd seen this tender gaze in the expressions of Z and D as we'd hunched over a tray of sand together and peeled back painful layers to my story. This look of love peeked through dozens of small moments on my journey. Whether it exuded from those who cared for me most deeply or was demonstrated through the kindness of strangers, every experience of *emblepo* pointed me back to grace.

I imagine all the clamor surrounding Peter went momentarily silent as he stared back at Jesus. Oh, the memories that must have flooded him. That moment on the Sea of Galilee when his gaze skittered from Jesus as his feet began slipping beneath the waves.

The brief pause when he took bread and fish from Jesus's hands before turning to pass it along to the multitudes. That day on the Mount of Transfiguration, when Jesus revealed to him the fullness of his identity. The intimate moments they had shared just a few hours ago during Passover.

Now he was seen in his shame. He'd been seen at his worst. In all the confusion and chaos of the moment, the loving gaze of Christ was fixed on him. That was the countenance of Jesus toward Peter, and toward the shame and rejection and floundering self-protection of a world set against him. Jesus looked on all those crowds screaming for his death and violently fixated on his death and loved them.

That is also his countenance toward you and me.

His invitation pulses through the pages of Scripture: Come. Taste and see and experience this God who tells us that we are his beloved *in the middle of the panic,* in all our anxiety and woundedness and sin and shame. He invites us to be seen here. To be known and loved and called to a different way of life. He invites us to become his beloved.

Peter in this moment is a prime representation of what it means to be human. Our most deeply ingrained tendency is to do what Peter did, over and over again. Panic, pain, insecurity, and shame still ruthlessly drive me to self-protection. A thousand different impulses can provoke us to run, hiding and grasping for our packaging. In a split second, that white-hot rush of anxiety can cause me to feel completely alone, rearing up in self-sufficiency and then wondering where Jesus has gone. I become consumed with projecting a more polished, less honest version of myself. That's where I was last week. In this tension is where God wants to meet us. Here, I keep asking for eyes to see what a life defined by love looks like.

Oh Jesus, would you help me see it?

That dark night marked a turning point in Peter's life. Moving forward, he is characterized by confident humility and quiet courage. Evidence of this transformation is tucked throughout the pages of Scripture. The book of Acts records the surprise of many when they witness his boldness, which is consistently linked to time spent in the presence of Jesus. Peter knew who he was, and he knew who God is. He'd experienced the truth that nothing in his life, *nothing at all*, was off-limits from God's unstoppable grace. His personal knowledge of Love gave him the courage to unwind his packaging and unbandage his wounds in public. He was fully known by God, and that gave him the freedom to be fully known by others, too.

Peter had discovered the secret of the kingdom: the glory of God bursts forth not from the strong ones but from the ones who know they are weak. His power hides itself in the lives of the wounded, unleashed in those who know who they are *and know who he is*. When I think about Peter, I rethink my definition of courage.

Maybe courage isn't the absence of anxiety, but the practice of trusting that we are loved and held no matter what.[2]

Over the last few years, I've discovered my battles with anxiety and anorexia can lead me in two directions. All the forces of hell storm the first direction, yanking me toward despair, self-pity, and resignation. Here, these ongoing battles serve the dark and convoluted purpose of the Enemy: to torment and afflict us, denigrating our dignity and fragmenting our sense of identity. He will use anything to make us question the transformation that is ours in Christ. The kingdom of darkness is bent on seeing us shrink back from the truth that we are unconditionally loved, triggering the shadows in us to be repelled from our deepest identity.

When I look at the emotional landscape of this generation, I see many of us entangled in his tactics. We're all determined to not be the weak ones, fiercely bent on pretending we're fine. We view our fragilities, limitations, and wounds as secrets to be hidden. Many of us feel a wild, often neurotic, need to distance ourselves from our insecurities in order to project a shinier and more flattering front. Deep down, we're terrified to be discovered for who we think we actually are. Our identity in Christ is meant to be our grounding, the steady foundation on which we build our lives. Without it, we live in an identity of our own crafting, built on the shaky illusion that we are what people say about us or do to us. This self-identity demands constant maintenance. As we constantly attempt to manipulate how others perceive us, our value becomes defined by those who like us and those who don't.

> We live in a world trying to force others to love the fake versions of ourselves.

But I've sensed God inviting me in an entirely different direction. He invites me to view my wounds and weaknesses in another way: not as problems to fix or secrets to hide, but places to encounter his presence. When I view these lingering struggles through the lens of Love, the Enemy's purposes lose power. These struggles no longer define me or have a voice in determining who I am, but rather become portals through which his glory and grace find full expression. They lead me not into hiding and isolation and shame, but toward greater intimacy and reliance on the One who has orchestrated every detail of my life according to his good and holy purpose.

God continually invites me to see and align my life around his idea of reality, which is very different than mine. According to him, we are graced and called and chosen when we are everything *but fine*. That's the message of the gospel. When we believe we are the beloved of God, rooting ourselves securely in that identity, we begin to experience transformation in every facet of our lives. It changes everything. That's when the floodgates of true healing break open. Suddenly, those wounded and fragmented parts of us don't threaten our sense of worth but become the very place where we can grow in the grace and knowledge of God. We don't feel that frantic urge to hide our scars anymore. Our striving ebbs as we begin to live from a place of *already being seen*.

On this pathway, confession becomes a declaration of freedom and vulnerability doesn't quicken us to run but drives us deeper into community. As we are released more and more from our bondage to fear, we are welcomed deep into the house of God, which is the house of Love. Like Peter, we find ourselves increasingly free to unwind ourselves of packaging and unbandage our wounds in public.

Fully known by God, we can be fully known by others, too.

I want to say yes to this direction with God. Yes to this identity. Yes to ever-deepening intimacy. But I'm learning that my yes to God means saying a continual no to all the other voices clamoring for my attention and to the torrent of the world's assumptions about who I am or should be or need to be. Saying yes to God means saying no to the packaging that shrouds the truth of my not enoughness. Saying yes to God means saying no to everything else that screams for my loyalty and repels me from identifying as the weak one.

Saying yes to God means releasing my compulsive tendencies to measure up, my running fear of what others think, and my obsessive need to position myself in the most flattering light. When I say yes to becoming the beloved, I say no to all other names I've come to define myself by and that have become the standard for how I measure my worth. When I choose to see through the lens of Love, perfectionism no longer serves to prevent failure but rather conceals the display of God's power through my life. Striving becomes counterproductive. People-pleasing is robbed of its purpose. But these inner impulses have formed the core of the person I've projected myself to be, which often feels like the very core of who I am. When I think about operating without these patterns, those words from the apostle Paul come to mind again: "Whenever you eat this bread and drink this cup, you are retelling the story, proclaiming our Lord's death until he comes" (1 Cor. 11:26 TPT).

Becoming the beloved not only means professing the death of Jesus but becoming an active participant in my own. There's a slow putting to death that takes place. A slaying of that fake version of myself that seeks approval and affirmation in the eyes of the world. As we continue to learn and grow into who God says we already are, he continually gives us eyes to see more and more of how we are operating in ways that don't reflect the truth of his Love. And he asks us to release those ways to him. Over and over and over again.

Noticing our emotions, responses, reactions, and thought patterns is the first way we say yes to becoming the beloved. Amid the distraction of our world and the disorder in our own inner lives, noticing can often feel at first like an underdeveloped muscle, awkward and uncomfortable to put into use. *But awareness is essential to healing and growth.* The unsettling relational interaction. Our unexpected spiral into insecurity. Our overblown reaction. The direction our thoughts ran in a moment of tension or uncertainty. These moments were never intended to be rushed past or piled over with coping mechanisms and distractions. When we slow down and begin to notice these moments littering our days, we unearth sacred opportunities to witness the Spirit of God, who promises to lead and guide us into all truth, at work in our lives (John 16:13).

Emotional awareness becomes a gift, creating space in the neural pathways of our brains to identify what's happening internally before we immediately move into dysregulation. Noticing creates an opportunity for connection with God *in the present moment*. Self-awareness becomes a tool of grace, helping us understand the deeper story of our lives. With clearer and more complete vision, we are able to recognize how our pasts have formed us and continue to resurface in the present. As we weave these practices in and throughout our lives, we invite Truth to reshape us and respond to God's invitation to wholeness. Slowly, with a wobbly and unsteady gait, we begin learning what it looks like to walk in the way of Love.

CHAPTER FIFTEEN

Becoming Us

If you came to this book numb and wounded, you are not the only one. I did, too. I had that numb feeling, like when your leg has fallen asleep, but right down to the deepest part of me. I couldn't feel anything. But then there's that tingling sensation that follows. It's uncomfortable. It's painful. But you know that whatever was asleep is waking up again. I pray that as you've encountered the grace that restores, you've begun to sense that tingling in your soul inviting you to come alive to hope. To beauty. To your own beating heart. And maybe, in that inner place that typically spins with a whirling knot of anxiety, you've seen glimpses of what it might feel like to be grounded and more present to life again.

Many of us have sat in church pews, some of us every Sunday since infancy, and have listened to those familiar words, "God loves you," over and over and over again. That was me. I heard that three-word phrase so many times the radical, life-changing truth of it lessened in meaning. Maybe that's you, too. Or maybe you didn't grow up in the church, but those words feel utterly confusing to you. When the pain of life rolled in like a thick and inescapable fog, it ripped the capacity to trust that Love right out of you, leaving you cold and empty and aching. Now those words just bounce off your intellect, unable to touch all the wounded places inside. That was me, too.

It's one thing to be told God loves you. Intellectual beliefs have little place to take root in us, much less shape a life whose thoughts, words, and actions reflect that truth. That kind of knowledge stays in your head, simply to be remembered and cognitively understood. It's another thing to have this knowledge pushed down into the emotional places of your heart, where it can heal and become a new foundation on which to build your life.[1] Only an experiential journey with Love himself can take the fact of his radical, unconditional affection and forge it into the very essence of who you are. That's what this book has been all about: offering some space and tools and words for this journey.

I was with Z and D again on one of my last days in treatment when they decided to introduce me to another unique form of therapy: equine therapy. This kind of therapy is experiential in nature, capitalizing on the connection between people and horses to enhance physical or emotional healing. Everyone who knows me well typically starts laughing at this point in the story. You see, I'm afraid of animals.

On this sticky July afternoon, however, I kept that piece of information to myself and soon found myself sitting on a faded couch in a small, air-conditioned office adjoining a barn, rigidly facing Z and D as I concentrated on a desk fan in the corner of the room. I could feel my body progressively tighten by the moment, as if every whirl of the fan wound my nerves tighter and tighter.

"Equine therapy revolves around metaphors," Z was saying. "Today, we'll be using a horse named Spirit." As he leaned forward, I watched him stroke his peppered-grey beard again. "Similar to sand tray therapy, we are going to pretend the arena is your world.

Spirit will be symbolic of something in your life. All other objects or people in the arena are available to you at your disposal."

I nodded. Once, twice, and then a third time.

Z smiled at me, his expression hinting of gentle humor. "Sound good? Now, remember. This is your world. You can do with it what you like." Pausing for another nod, he chuckled softly as he stood, "Then put your boots on and we'll get started."

After pulling on knee-high boots rimmed with mud, I followed Z and D out the doors into the arena. The smell of fresh hay and horse manure soaked me in a pungent, nostril-flooding wave as we walked toward a large, shaded opening. My gaze quickly located a horse standing in the middle of the arena. Stuffing my hands in my pockets, I chewed on my lip as Z walked over to her. I watched him rest a hand on her flank, scratching her behind the ears and whispering softly into her ear before turning toward me once again.

"This is Spirit . . ." he told me in a low tone, pointing to a light blue bridle hooked on the fence nearest to me. "Your job is to put that bridle on Spirit and lead her around the arena."

As if sensing my caution, D slipped the bridle off its hook and handed it to me. "You can do this. Just go up to her quietly. Act like you're in control and slip it over her head."

I attempted gingerly. Once, twice, three times. Spirit bucked and I scurried backward, eyes growing glassy as an unexpected surge of helplessness engulfed me. Visibly flustered, I sensed Z realized that something deeper had been triggered.

"Let's stop for a moment," he said. His calming voice soothed my frayed nerves. After a long silence, he asked me softly, "In your life, what do you think Spirit represents?"

I stared at the horse, a heaviness settling as I slowly ticked off the reasons why I'd spent the last ten weeks in treatment. I looked at Z and then looked back at Spirit, "I feel so out of control. I don't know what she's going to do and I can't stop her." Warmth crawled up my spine as my words spilled. They possessed deeper layers of meaning than I'd intended to reveal.

"Okay, good job." Z didn't engage further. Taking the bridle, he handed me Spirit's lead rope instead. "Let's try leading Spirit around the arena."

I took the rope and attempted to tug the horse forward. "Come on, Spirit," I begged. "Come on. Just follow me, please." Spirit tugged in the opposite direction. I tugged back. She snapped at my hand. I jumped, startled.

"What are you feeling?" D asked me.

I stared at her, speechless. But my body knew. It pulsated with those all-too-familiar feelings that had consumed my life the past several years: the rush of clammy and sickening anxiety. That spiraling feeling of helplessness, sucking me into an emotional black hole without my permission or control. I tugged on Spirit's lead rope again. "Come on Spirit, *please . . .*" I whispered. She snapped at my hand again as my voice cracked.

"Taylor, stop." D called from across the room. "What do you need right now?"

I turned, swallowing hard. *"Can you walk with me?"*

D's lips curved into a smile. Coming up alongside me, she gently placed her palms on mine and guided my hands into a different position. Her presence steadied me as I tugged on Spirit again. The horse took a step. And then another. The three of us kept pace together as we inched around the arena. Muscles loosening, I began to exhale. I was doing it, wasn't I? Was I getting better? But just as the breath began seeping from my lungs, Spirit came to a sudden halt. Looking me in the eye, she reared, coming up on her hind legs with a force that I wasn't prepared to handle.

"Eyes on me, Taylor! Eyes on me!"

Z yelled from across the arena, his gaze locked on me. I stilled as my gaze found his. Fiercely holding eye contact, I slowly guided

Spirit toward him as my tears began to stream, slowly at first and then more steadily as his words penetrated deep. With no question in my mind, I knew Z's call that day was the words of Jesus toward me. Toward *us*. Gradually, I've come to see that the arena on that July afternoon is an unmistakable picture of this journey, the relationship between D and me a ringing testament to the power and beauty of community.

> The work of the Enemy will always try to keep
> us locked in the silent anguish of isolation.

He wants us to hide in shame. That's been his aim since his slithering work in the garden of Eden. Isolation is often paradoxical in nature, causing us to feel raw with loneliness *while at the same time* terrified of exposure. Our sense of shame narrows our vision. Slowly, the wounds we hide become the only things we see. The longer we stay in this place, the more we perceive the pain braided throughout our stories as uncommonly exclusive to our experience rather than the mutual thread intersecting every human life. Isolation drives us deeper behind the thick walls of self-protection.

But the way of Love is always a way of invitation. Relationship is the beating heart of God, continually calling us to join him in our places of shame, anxiety, and pain. He gently asks us the same question he asked Adam and Eve: "*Where are you?*" He welcomes our woundedness. Our weakness. Our wrestling. Rather than removing our scars, he shows us his own. Grace offers us a safe space to be held in all our darkness, and to be seen by a God who doesn't flinch or turn away when we unbandage our real selves. We no longer need to hide or live in isolation; it's safe to bring all our struggles and insecurities into God's loving presence.

However, during the darkest years of my struggles with anxiety and anorexia, I didn't trust that Love. I didn't trust anyone's love. The longer I kept the truth of my struggles from others, the more suspicious I became toward anyone who came too close. Casual questions from people who cared suddenly felt terrifyingly threatening. But therapists like Z and D, as well as many others, continually met my resistance with compassion. Over and over again, they showed me they cared about my honesty. In fact, they were committed to it. Gradually, I began to feel freer to take my shame, fears, and struggles out of isolation and into the hands of those who could hold and receive them.

Here, I began to experience the power of another person's presence in my pain. I began to witness the ways human connection dismantles shame. I was seen and not alone. With the therapeutic help of others, I slowly began to reconnect to my experiences and to the emotions running through my body. I realized all those feelings I'd feared weren't quite as scary as I thought. And the more I joined God in this inner work, the more I realized *I had never been alone.* Echoes of his faithfulness reverberated throughout my story, giving evidence of his presence in moments where I'd previously felt abandoned.

I've come to see that this journey is characterized by relationship: not only with God *but with each other.* This road was never intended to be walked alone, but a road on which we link arms with others on the same journey. That's how we stay awake to Love, calling us to fix our eyes on the One whose eyes are already fixed on us.

> Community has always been the
> crucible of transformation.

I imagine, however, that some of us have gnawing hesitancies, and maybe even deep wounds, inflicted by the community of

Christ. Too many of us have heard about God's love from church pews but have never experienced the transformation and intimacy of Love himself. Only time spent on this inward journey can soften our sharp edges to live, love, and lead from a more healed place. Some have sat in those church pews and heard spiritual leaders exhort them to love one another. But they feel deadened inside, both seething with anger and drowning in shame. They've experienced the razor-sharp edges of abuse from people who were supposed to be safe, maybe even from that very person standing on the platform and preaching love. "Forgive and forget," they've heard said. "You just need to pray about it," they've been told. These cutting, insensitive remarks can feel so much more confusing and wounding when they come from people who profess Christ.

The sharp and unhealed places in us, void of grace, often form the tight spaces and rigid structures that fracture our churches. Maybe you've felt this divide, like a knife that cut deep and caused you to feel safer struggling in silence. Or maybe you've never been hurt by the church. But when you slip into Sunday morning gatherings filled with neat rows of smiling people, you wonder if your pain is welcome here. *Does my story still hold value when I'm in the middle of a mess? When I'm angry and questioning and doubting God's goodness?*

We spend so much time telling other people how they need to change, proving ourselves right, and shouting what we think God has for someone else that we have little time left to discover what he has for us. When we haven't acknowledged, owned, and received grace for our own brokenness, we have little capacity to allow each other to be broken too. We judge the filth and weakness of those around us, pointing fingers toward others and away from the insecurity and shame we feel about ourselves. Today, our churches can tell a narrative that silently labels weakness as an inconvenience and woundedness as a detraction from the cross.

That kind of narrative leaves little room for healing or connection. It simply perpetuates hiding and shame.

But the story of the kingdom rings with a different reality. Over and over again, we see the biblical narrative advanced through broken people, well aware of their scars and insufficiencies, yet committed to walking in the way of Love. The biblical story points to a beautiful reality where brokenness is our greatest qualification, and where we are each graced and chosen to be used in a significant way, not through our giftedness *but through our wounds.*

This inward journey always leads us out into self-sacrifice rather than self-sufficiency. We are called to weave our time, presence, and unique experiences of Love in and throughout the journeys of others. When we've experienced light in our own dark places, we can begin to walk light into others' darkness. When we've tasted the spaciousness of true freedom, we can hold more space for the unfixed parts of another. When we've breathed deeply of Love, we can exhale defensiveness when offended, allowing grace to define our responses. We can become the kind of people who walk alongside others without needing anything from them, offering a steady presence *as they join God* in their own places of pain. It's those of us who've seen God in our scars that can freely offer them up as places where others see God.

> Part of experiencing the love of God is seeing and feeling that love embodied in one another.

Community is where Love becomes a tangible expression rather than a theoretical concept. It's through connection with others in our shame, the compassionate presence of others in our pain, and companionship with others on the same journey that we become his beloved, together. *That's the invitation for you and for me.* For those of us who've been wounded to join this biblical story, reminding the church of the cost of grace. And compelling them to stand with us under the cross of Christ, where we can all gaze on the nail-scarred truth that the most powerful work of God was unleashed through healed wounds. Here, and only here, can we cultivate communities that reflect that truth.

Living in community is complicated. We're so used to skin-deep smiles and small talk that this slow, messy, true community can often feel foreign to us. I like my relationships to be tidy and predictable, and those qualities quickly unravel when we plunge beneath pleasantries and good eye contact. True community, deep and authentic connection, means bruised knees and sore muscles. Steady patience and repetitive actions. It's a slow, not instant, love. It requires me to stay in the awkwardness, linger in the discomfort, and lean into the hard conversations with those who see all the worst parts of me.

When the masks are peeled, I've quickly discovered that "I'm fine" is no longer a viable answer. People see the real me, under all the packaging and charm and pretty smiles, and they realize that I'm not quite as together as I seemed. Oftentimes, my mess triggers their own and, suddenly, our insecurities begin arguing with each other. True community reveals how quickly I can get offended and how quickly I can offend others. It requires both confession and forgiveness: showing up, coming clean, being seen, and giving grace over and over again. It requires the self-awareness to see myself as I really am, to see others as they really are, and the humility to openly acknowledge both. It requires less advice and more understanding. Less solutions, more empathy.

While the most powerful work of God is unleashed through healed wounds, the most powerful work of the Enemy leaks from unhealed wounds. Darkness is constantly trying to pit us against each other. Divide. Split. Create conflict. Speak poorly about the other person to make ourselves feel better. True community requires sacrifice and commitment to each other. The kind of bulletproof commitment that doesn't rescind with tension but *runs toward it*, more intent on restoration than being proven right. This kind of commitment pursues healing, even if that means getting hurt in the process. Grace must always sit at the core of our shared experiences, cultivating a safe space where trust runs deep, truth is spoken, and people are fiercely committed to the growth of each other.

That's how true community is built.

That's the kind of community I long to live in. That I want to fight for. And that I pray we each feel a fire burning inside us to cultivate. This process of "becoming us" isn't perfect, but it's beautiful. It's the place where I've begun to find healing and where I've seen hope again. Although I certainly still struggle and often fail to live out the message of this book, I've seen that every moment of this journey has been worth it. *Especially that moment on the bathroom floor.* My struggles and wounds that initially drove me into isolation have slowly granted me sacred permission to sit beside the darkness of others and offer hope.

The one thing I don't like about books is that they always have an ending, which can often feel like the finish line to this journey we've taken together. You and I can be tempted to strain for instant change. A quick before-and-after. But the truth is, these last few moments together are simply the starting line. The starting line for a journey that begins by admitting, "I'm not fine." A phrase that, hopefully, both of us now realize isn't as scary as it once seemed.

Notes

Chapter One

[1] Brené Brown, *The Gifts of Imperfection: Let Go of Who You Think You're Supposed to Be and Embrace Who You Are* (Center City, MN: Hazelden, 2010), 68.

Chapter Two

[1] Insight taken from an interview with clinical mental health counselor Rachel Elmore.

[2] Annie F. Downs, "Episode 328: John Mark Comer + Live No Lies," in *That Sounds Fun*, podcast, MP3audio, 01:12:42, accessed June 17, 2022, https://www.anniefdowns.com/podcast/episode-328-john-mark-comer-live-no-lies/.

[3] Sissy Goff, *Raising Worry-Free Girls: Helping Your Daughter Feel Braver, Stronger, and Smarter in an Anxious World* (Bloomington, MN: Bethany House, 2019), 25.

[4] K. J. Ramsey, *This Too Shall Last: Finding Grace When Suffering Lingers* (Grand Rapids: Zondervan, 2020), 140.

[5] Ramsey, *This Too Shall Last*, 55.

[6] Vocabulary.com, s.v. "rejection," https://www.vocabulary.com/dictionary/rejection.

[7] Henri Nouwen, *Following Jesus: Finding Our Way Home in an Age of Anxiety* (London: SPCK, 2019), 98.

Chapter Three

[1] Some of the above descriptions were taken from Sharon Salszberg's Mindful.org article "How to Recognize Your Inner Critic," May 3, 1018, https://www.mindful.org/how-to-recognize-your-inner-critic/.

[2] Andrew Peterson, vocalist, "Be Kind to Yourself," written by Andrew Peterson and Gabe Scott, track 8 on *The Burning Edge of Dawn*, Centricity Music, 2015, compact disc.

[3] Adam Young, "Warfare Part 7: The Modern Screwtape Letters," *The Place We Find Ourselves*, podcast, Dec. 16, 2019, MP3 audio, 21:08, https://adamyoungcounseling.com/2019/12/29/warfare-part-7-the-modern-screwtape-letters/.

Chapter Four

[1] *Merriam-Webster*, s.v. "self-deception," https://www.merriam-webster.com /dictionary/self-deception.

Chapter Five

[1] Roy Hession, *The Calvary Road*, 3rd ed. (Fort Washington, PA: CLC, 2017), 21.

[2] Encyclopedia.com, s.v. "sacred space," http://www.encyclopedia.com /environment/encyclopedias-almanacs-transcripts-and-maps/sacred-space.

[3] Beth Guckenberger, *Start with Amen: How I Learned to Surrender by Keeping the End in Mind* (Nashville: Thomas Nelson, 2017), 39—emphasis in original.

Chapter Six

[1] John Piper, "'The Word of God: Living, Active, Sharp," Desiring God, September 8, 1996, http://www.desiringgod.org/messages/the-word-of-god -living-active-sharp.

[2] C. H. Spurgeon, "The Sword of the Spirit," sermon (no. 2201), Metropolitan Tabernacle Newington, April 19, 1891, London, UK, Blue Letter Bible, http:// www.blueletterbible.org/Comm/spurgeon_charles/sermons/2201.cfm.

[3] Much of following section on agreements is drawn from Adam Young, "Warfare Part 3: Agreements," *The Place We Find Ourselves*, podcast, July 29, 2019, MP3 audio, 27:00, https://theplacewefindourselves.libsyn.com/47-warfare -part-6-breaking-agreements.

[4] Young, "Warfare Part 3: Agreements."

[5] These insights are adapted from Curt Thompson, *Anatomy of the Soul: Surprising Connections between Neuroscience and Spiritual Practices That Can Transform Your Life and Relationships* (Carol Stream, IL: Tyndale, 2010), 65–78.

Chapter Seven

[1] *Cambridge Dictionary*, s.v. "put on a brave face," http://www.dictionary .cambridge.org/us/dictionary/english/put-on-a-brave-face.

[2] Paraphrased from John Lynch, *The Cure: What If God Isn't Who You Think He Is and Neither Are You?* (Dawsonville, GA: Trueface, 2016), 90.

Chapter Eight

[1] Ramsey, *This Too Shall Last,* 32

[2] Gerald G. May, *Addiction and Grace: Love and Spirituality in the Healing of Addictions* (New York: HarperCollins, 2007), 106.

[3] Shauna Niequist, *Present over Perfect: Leaving behind Frantic for a Simpler, More Soulful Way of Living* (Grand Rapids: Zondervan, 2016), 38.

Chapter Nine

[1]One book that helped me understand my wounded self is Brennan Manning, *Abba's Child: The Cry of the Heart for Intimate Belonging* (Colorado Springs: Navpress, 1997).

Chapter Ten

[1]Aundi Kolber, *Try Softer: A Fresh Approach to Move Us out of Anxiety, Stress, and Survival Mode—and into a Life of Connection and Joy* (Carol Stream, IL: Tyndale, 2020), 100.

[2]Kolber, *Try Softer*, 100.

[3]Paraphrased from Henri Nouwen, *Life of the Beloved: Spiritual Living in a Secular World* (New York: Crossroad, 2002).

[4]For more on healthy rhythms of entering God's presence and going out into the world, see Beth Guckenberger, *Reckless Faith: Let Go and Be Led* (Grand Rapids: Zondervan: 2008), 21–22.

Chapter Eleven

[1]Online Etymology Dictionary, s.v. "wait," http://www.etymonline.com/word/wait.

[2]David Benner, *The Gift of Being Yourself: The Sacred Call to Self-Discovery* (Downers Grove, IL: InterVarsity Press, 2004), 59.

Chapter Twelve

[1]May, *Addiction and Grace*, 4.

[2]May, *Addiction and Grace*, 133.

[3]Annie F. Downs, "Episode 327: Curt Thompson + Soul of Desire," *That Sounds Fun*, podcast, MP3 audio, 56.50, http://www.anniefdowns.com/podcast/episode-327-curt-thompson-soul-of-desire/.

Chapter Fourteen

[1]Thomas L. Constable, "Notes on the Gospel of Luke," SonicLight.com, 2021, https://www.planobiblechapel.org/tcon/notes/html/nt/luke/luke.htm.

[2]Ramsey, *This Too Shall Last*, 213.

Chapter Fifteen

[1]For an excellent podcast on these themes, see Tyler Staton, "Prayer Training," uploaded May 25, 2021, 51:03, http://www.vimeo.com/554859665.